The First Book of
Irish Myths and Legends

EOIN NEESON

THE MERCIER PRESS
4 BRIDGE STREET, CORK

© Eoin Neeson, 1965

Third printing 1970
Eight edition 1982
Ninth edition 1984

ISBNO 85342 1307

A 80328

398.232415

Printed by Litho Press Co., Midleton, Co. Cork.

Contents

Introduction

For the most part the origins of the Irish people are known only through such delightful but vague assumptions as this:

'Long, long ago beyond the misty space of twice a thousand
years,
In Erin old there dwelt a mighty race, taller than Roman
spears',

which is taken from the poem 'The Celts' by Thomas D'Arcy Mc Gee. Otherwise myth, legend and quasi history combine to give an indistinct impression of Firbolg, Tuatha de Danaan and Milesian forebears with, depending largely on the personal whim of the author, hardly a single verifiable fact or substantial theory about any one of them. The result is, of course, that a number of responsible people – many of whom should know better – have rejected the idea that Firbolg, Tuatha de Danaan or Milesian ever existed in this country at all, and cautiously confine their observations to the people known to have flourished in, or just prior to, recorded history, rather as if the Celtic people, like some preposterous legion of Minervas sprung fully grown and fully armed from the head of Zeus, overnight populated the face of Ireland with a society of considerable sophistication.

Such an attitude is regrettable if only because it is as assumptive as – and considerably less provocative than – those which support belief in the existence of these ancient peoples. The real pity, however, is that a considerable volume of evidence, circumstantial though it may be, surrounding their origin and coming to Ireland has not, to my knowledge, been simply assembled and published en masse together with some of the legends in support of the belief, before.

The difficulty is where to begin. Since this book concerns myths and mythical figures, perhaps mythology is a good point at which to start. Most dictionaries will generally define a myth as a purely fictitious narrative often involving super-

7

natural or supra-natural persons and embodying popular ideas on natural phenomena. But historians, archaeologists and ethnologists are putting a new interpretation on myths, particularly since the German, von Schliemann, discovered the site of so-called "mythical" Troy at the beginning of the century, and so upset the convenient notion that it was all a figment of Homer's imagination.

Scientific archaeology has proved that a city existed on the site of Troy — in fact that several cities preceded it — and that it was great and walled; that it was destroyed by fire about the time in which Homer set the Trojan wars. The question now often asked is where does myth end and truth begin? One wonders if the question should not be at what point does imagination cloak the truth with a supra-mundane stature?

Because of the larger-than-life nature of myths and the nature of the characters in them, the tendency has been to dismiss the notion that they have any factual origin — I am not, need I add, referring to deistic concepts with quite another sort of origin. But surely their larger-than-lifeness is in itself an indication of the factual origin of myths and heroic legends — however tangential that fact may be? We all know the good storyteller; the man in the bar, in the drawing room, in the restaurant who has an eager audience listening to his latest yarn. We know that the truth upon which the story rests is liable to artistic mutation in the interests of dramatic presentation; but we also know that veracity doet not give way completely to fiction, even though special emphasis has been added here and here. The same is almost always true of any incident retold — by you, by your neighbour, by a newspaper reporter; any newspaper reporter will tell you how simple it is to tell the same story half a dozen times with a different emphasis each time — many of them do it every day when writing for a number of newspapers. But the essential facts remain.

The second important consideration here is the nature of what was happening as these stories proliferated and became myths. It was this: men were telling each other by word of mouth what had gone before them — for they had few and extremely difficult means of written communication, and even then it was confined to a tiny minority. They were not at that time particularly interested in inventing and telling each other stories for their own sake; this is a refined social entertainment that belongs to a later social development. They were recounting the greatness of those who went before them. In other words they were passing history from one generation to the next. If the characters in that history grew disproportionately large under the influence of time and many virile imaginations, and if the events in which they figured grew with them, who, knowing the man in the bar, will wonder overmuch at it? And who will assert that truth and fact, as a consequence, are altogether absent from these heroic people and their activities?

Europe has inherited two main streams of mythology, subdivided, in turn, roughly in two. They are the dark, sombre, brooding mythological cycle of Scandinavia and Germany and the bright, sun-filled (irrespective of how much blood was spilled) Greco-Roman tradition. So far as Ireland is concerned and in spite of her geographical location, she shares in her myths the sunshine and brightness of the Greek and Roman tales. Not only does she share an essence of feeling in her myths with those of Attica, but many comparable incidents, style and characters as well, as we shall see. Why?

Isolated on the very fringe of Europe, lapped by the nethermost ocean of the period, and a good deal closer – in the physical sense at least – to the hairy primitives of Britain, Germany and Scandinavia and their bloody sagas of immolation and savage despair, why were the Irish evidently of a considerably more advanced social and ethnological stage of development, and why are their myths and stories permeated with the same light and brilliance to be found in the Greek and Roman? Perhaps in seeking the answer to these questions we may also find a clue to the origin of the people themselves.

To begin with the Milesians lived, somewhere about 2,000 to 3,000 B.C. – and possibly earlier – in Ionia and were, according to Herodotus, an Hellenic and Phoenician people speaking a distinctive language of their own and, it is thought, with even older Scythian connections. They were a strong, independent people of distinctive characteristics so much so that they were the only ones of that region – roughly the western coastline of modern Turkey – from whom neither Croesus the Lydian nor Cyrus the Persian exacted tribute when they overran the area about 1,000 B. C. Both Herodotus and Xenophon mention the Milesians as being good at both commerce and war. They were also natural colonisers.

The Ionic Milesians (for what it is worth consider the aural similarity between Ionia, an Hellenic placename, and Cliona one of the names allegedly given to Ireland by her Milesian settlers, and later transmuted into the name of a mythical queen) lived in three cities the chief of which was called Miletus, but they represented only a portion of the race. The remainder were nomads – sea nomads at that – and settlers. It was, in fact, the Milesian command of the sea that enabled them to survive when their neighbours were destroyed by the Lydians, the Medes and the Persians; and it was their command of the sea that enabled them to establish trading colonies and permanent settlements in Sicily, Sardinia, Italy and Spain.

In the Leabhar Gabhala, the Book of Invasions, the seventh century pioneer attempt at a definitive historical study of the origins of the Irish race, the Milesians are represented as coming directly from Spain, which is utterly consistent with the Ionic Milesian colonisation of Sicily, Sardinia, Italy and Spain – Tartessia. What more natural places for westward probing colonists following the paths of (or it may be the stories about) earlier travellers such as Nemed and the Tuatha de Danaan to use as bases?

Now, although the Milesians like the Macedonians were Hellenes though not necessarily Greeks, with the same religious tradition, they lived in Asia among nations that to them were barbaric and, in the pantheistic climate of the period, undoubtedly came under the influence of Asiatic mystical beliefs (as indeed Herodotus remarks), a point which will become significant in a moment. Furthermore it is known that both the Milesians and the Lydians had a common tongue, like that of the Macedonians of Hyperborean – or barbaric – origin, which could, indeed, have been a Celtic tongue. That it was Indo-European is undisputed.

In the Newgrange tumulus, Co. Meath, in Ireland, there is a sacrificial altarstone above which a symbol is carved in a rock. This symbol, of the sun, is identical with the symbol ascribed to the sun-god of the Phoenicians of the Mediterranean at the period.

We know that the Milesians lived, probably between the years 4,000 B. C. and 200 B. C., in Asia Minor. We know that they were brave soldiers, clever merchants and traders and prosperous husbandmen and, above all, seafarers, adventurers and colonisers of distinction... indeed so noteworthy was their prowess in this direction that they were in a position to offer Sardinia to Cyrus, the Persian, on one occasion.

We know that in Newgrange in Ireland there is an emblem in a four thousand years old tumulus which is identical with emblems commonplace in the region of Ionia where the Milesian cities were flourishing four thousand years ago.

In addition we know the following:

After the battle of Mycale, in which the confederate Hellenic states defeated the invading army of Xerxes, the Milesians who had been an occupied people under Persian domination at this time, attacked their enemies from the rear during the battle and 'proved their bitterest enemies' (Herodotus; Histories, Book 9).

Subsequently the Hellenes held a council on the future of the people of Ionia and decided to abandon the indefensible coast to the Persians, and remove the Ionians for re-settlement elsewhere. The plan was eventually abandoned (after pressure from the Athenians who had no wish to see this forward area of defence fall into the hands of the enemy) but not before two things happened; a confederation of Pelloponesians was formed for Ionian defence, and many of the Milesians – the most prosperous and adventurous of the Ionians – decided to ship westward and settle in their new colonies elsewhere. One wonders if they did not by this time have a colony beyond the Hesperides too?

We are also told, of course, that whatever about the Firbolgs (and it is hard to escape the impression that scholars have reservations about consigning them also to the limbo of strict myth, if only because of the surpassing evidence of their own eyes that many still seem to survive to-day) the Milesians and the Tuatha de Danaan are figments of the Celtic imagination. So far as the Milesians are concerned there is, judging from what has been written above, at least a substantive case on foot of their being seafarers, traders, colonisers and warriors; and a reasonably circumstantial case in support of the theory that they came to Ireland at about the time conjectured.

So much for that; we are told in addition that the Milesians came to Ireland (about) 2,000 B. C.; that they followed the Tuatha da Danaan who, in turn, had followed the Nemedians and either conquered or absorbed the, more or less, indigenous Firbolg/Fomorian inhabitants. We are told that the Firbolgs were uncouth, savage and altogether unfit specimens for association with the mystical and visionary Tuatha de Danaan; in effect that they were very much like the Picts who flourished until much later in the neighbouring island, succumbing finally to the resources of civilisation in the guise, on one hand, of the Roman legions and, on the other, of warlike Irish settlers who conquered Argyle and subsequently most of Scotland. The enigma up to now has been the disparity of views about the identity of the Celts or Gaels, who are supposed to have had no established connection with the Mediterranean. But most views, however they might have differed from each other in argument, generally had a passing reference in common to which few paid any real attention; and this was mentioned in a great number of Irish traditions of the Scythians. These references in the old Irish tales have generally been dismissed as mere intrusive embellishments of later scribes letting their imaginations run wild, or have been passed over without comment; a few scholars, such as Mary Hutton, have paid them serious attention. And the results are intriguing at least. If the Scythians and the Celts should happen to have been a common people, innumerable contradictions would be resolved. And there is substantial evidence to suggest that they were related if not the same people. Miscellaneous, but contributary pieces of evidence may be found scattered throughout various works by different authorities. The Four Masters, for example, mention that after the Gaels (Celts) had arrived in Spain from Scythia, one of them, Bregan, built a tower and a city called after him, Bregantia. From the tower his son, Ith, saw Ireland in the distance. Red Hugh O'Donnell is alleged to have visited the site of the tower in 1602 A. D. Incidentally Ith, according to Padraic Colum, was the brother of one Mil or Mileadh, and the father of Eber and Eremon; this information is given with a slight variation in the Leabhar Gabhala. Colum adds, with it seems

12

to me several centuries of anticipation, that Mil equates with the Latin 'miles' soldier, and that Eber and Eremon both mean Irishman in Latin.

Be that as it may it seems to be stretching plausibility excessively in an unnecessary direction sinse we already know that the Milesians and the Celts flourished simultaneously in several parts of the world – Asia Minor, Italy and Spain; there is no dispute about that. The points is were the Milesians Celts? Could they have been Celts? The answer would appear to be that they could. They could certainly have been Scythians. It is by no means improbable that the Milesians were of Celtic extraction, at it seems the Macedonians, may have been also an Hellenic people. Herodotus (Histories, Book 1) states that the Macedonians, the Milesians, the Lydians and the Carians spoke a common language which was neither Greek nor Persian: Gaelic possibly. In support of this one further small point. It is established that the Scythians entered Asia in pursuit of the Cimmerians *whom they expelled from Europe.* In other words the Scythians drove these Cimmerians, as the Greeks called them, eastwards from the very area dominated by the Celts, who are also known to have gone eastwards and established a substantial colony in Asia. Is it possible that the Scythians and the Celts are one and the same, or at all events that the Scythians are of Celtic origin? Furthermore, having dealt with the Cimmerians and established themselves on the shores of the Caspian sea (to which many references also appear in the Irish legends and traditions), the Scythians drove southwards and subjugated the Medes, dominating the very territory in which the Milesians and Lydians were to flourish. The Scythians maintained their supremacy in that part of Asia for twenty-eight years, until the Medes again expelled them from it. But during that time Scythian customs, manners and traditions, not to mention blood, would have become firmly established – particularly as the vast tract of land known as Scythia was just north of Macedonia and its neighbour in Asia Minor, Ionia. It is only right to point out here that the Scythians, or Scoloti, originated according to one account of Herodotus (Hist. 4.7), when Hercules came to the region from his home on an island, *near Gades in the ocean beyond the Pillars of Hercules,* called Erythea, and cohabited with a snake woman

13

who bore three sons who were the forerunners of the Scythians.

The case for the Tuatha de Danaan is similar, but necessarily more conjectural. And little can be conjectured about them with safety; more, however, can be conjectured than has already been done with accuracy. For example the proper name of the Greeks, Danaos, may not be totally without significance in this context; but even more potent would appear to be a race mentioned by Xenophon, and possessing the same mystical, awe inspiring, wizardlike characteristics as the Tuatha de Danaan; they were called the Dana. And, as is well known, the proper title of Lugh Lamh Fada, son of the de Danaan hero Kian and of a royal Firbolg mother was the Il-Dana.

In addition, tradition has it that the Firbolgs were defeated on two seperate occasions – at the first and second battles of Moytura by the Tuatha de Danaan. On the second occasion we were given to understand that the Il-Dana, striding out of the west, came to the assistance of the Tuatha de Danaan and struck out (with the weapon of his long arm, perhaps) the remaining eye of that old and unpleasant Firbolg king, Balor of the Evil Eye, (the eyelid of whose maleficent optic, which had similar powers to those of the Medusa, was even then being propped conveniently open to exterminate what was left of the de Danaan; instead it admitted the Il-Dana's weapon, with fatal results for Balor... who happened to be his grandfather).

It is hardly too far fetched to read into this the intermingling, on the eastern – or most readily settled – coast, of established Firbolg and incoming Tuatha de Danaan communities... the Il-Dana, product of a de Danaan king and a Firbolg queen... clearly the sophisticated, mystical, but not necessarily excessively warlike Tuatha de Danaan would expand across the country. Equally clearly the Firbolgs would sooner or later find a common purpose in opposition... perhaps with ever increasing necessity, hence the two battles of Moytura... and face the Tuatha de Danaan in battle. Is it not likely that the coming of the Il-Dana to the assistance of the latter is merely a synonym for the fact that the uncommitted and intermarried Firbolgs of the east gave them their assistance at a critical moment? Such has been the pattern of battles won by invading settlers throughout history.

Finally, in this context, the Il-Dana is known to have brought with him a great light, generally supposed to come from his forehead, as well as his new weapon, indicated by long arm (Lamh Fada). Was the brightness that of one of the earliest bronze helmets seen in Ireland? Was the Lamh Fada, the long arm, a spear thrower, such as used by the Australian aboriginals to-day... and used almost exclusively, according to Xenophon, by the Asiatic communities of which the Dana were one?

In this context Irish tradition has it that the first known invader of Ireland from the far world was one Nemed (according to the Leabhar Gabhala). He found the country, or the inhabited part of it, occupied by Fomorians, a nomadic race of sea rovers indigenous to the northern world, rather like the Vikings some thousands of years later. The Nemedians were absorbed by these wild men. Nemed and his followers are said to have hailed from the region of the Caspian Sea... the very region in which Xenophon places the Danaans.

It is accepted by the Greeks and their historians, notably Herodotus, that the Scythians – known generally as Scoloti, by no means excessively removed from the Scotii by which the Irish became known – and the Celts, while undoubtedly to their minds Hyperboreans, or barbarians (so, we must remember, were all others except Greeks, including the Persians), were of a social and intellectual order much more advanced than their Germanic, Helvetian and Asiatic neighbours; they spoke, it is emphasised, an Indo-European language and maintained a large colony in Asia Minor which *retained its Celtic language into the fourth century* a.d.

The point I wish to emphasise is; so far Celtic scholars and historians have worked on the assumption that, if the Nemedians, the Tuatha de Danaan and the Milesians existed at all, they had widely different and separate origins. This is surely absurdly assumptive reasoning, particularly if one knows that the de Danaans, with many similar characteristics to the mysterious and magically inclined Dana, are like the Nemedians who preceded them reputed to have come from Asia Minor, as did the Milesians who followed them. And is it not an historic fact, as many historical examples show, that

15

colonisation from one source tends to attract successive waves of colonists from the same source rather than from alternative sources? It seems that this is not an unreasonable proposition. Of the Fomorians and the Firbolgs, little is said or conjectured, particularly of the former; and for a very good reason. They ware nomads, but not settlers. The Firbolgs who were not absorbed by the learned and scientifically minded Tuatha de Danaan perished; the Milesians, practical, hard-headed merchants, colons par excellence and warriors to boot, had little difficulty in supplanting the esoterically inclined de Danaan and taking the conduct of affairs out of their hands, leaving them their superstitions, their mysteries and their magic, all of which the Milesians would have held in some awe. Nevertheless it is hardly surprising that tradition holds, perhaps of this very situation, that the Tuatha de Danaan vanished, with their mysteries, under the earth where they still survive (or did at the time of earliest recorded history anyway) in the form of Sidhe, or fairy people. It is not hard to equate this belief with the gradual absorbtion of mystics like the de Danaan by a more vigorous and pragmatic people, who in turn must have benefitted from their forerunners by a great heightening of the imaginative and creative faculties.

The de Danaans occupied the country more or less peaceably, so far as one knows, until the coming of the Milesians. And here again I would put forward a suggestion entirely new in this context, but by no means hostile to the proposition I have already made; that the Nemedians, the de Danaans and the Milesians had a common origin, a common tongue and were very much kith if not indeed kin.

The Milesians, the final and lasting settlers, remained. It is my suggestion that they were not, as is generally held, only followed by the Gaels (Celts)... iw indeed they were... but were preceded by them. I propose that the Nemedians, following Partholon, and the Tuatha de Danaan, following the Nemedians were Celts and/or Scythians or both, and that the Milesians, living in close association with the Celts/Scythians in Asia Minor, and being settlers and colonisers in their own right, as well as better soldiers, administrators and traders than either, merely followed them as Milesians.

Nor does it follow that if the Nemedians, the Tuatha de Danaan and the Milesians displayed different characteristics

16

that they must have had separate racial origins. Time, particularly in a period of rapid mutation, emphasises contradictory facets of the same species; furthermore Scythia was so enormous that local conditions and influences could have produced widely different characteristics in people of the same ethnological and linguistic group.

Finally, on this point, there is a school of thought which holds that the name Ireland – Eire – is derived from Piera, a name with an Indo-European root expressing fertility or fecundity. It is known, of course, that the rich countryside of Ireland was regarded with something amounting to awe by the Greeks because of its fruitfulness. The Greek home of the Muses is also Piera. From this word, it is argued, is derived Eiru, Hibernia and Juvernia – all names for Ireland.

Before turning to a more immediate consideration of the Irish myths, and in particular of those in this book, here is what the Book of Invasions has to tell us about the early conquest of Ireland... dates, need I add, are still the subject of much controversy.

First to lead a colony to Ireland, immediately after the flood, was one Partholon, who, like those determined settlers who followed him, came from the cradle of the world, Asia Minor. Partholon apparently suffered his fate at the hands of the Fomorians or some other indigenous people, for nothing more is heard of him. Then came Nemed and his people, who once again were absorbed by the Fomorians – a sort of race of Calibans, it seems, who never took to anyone except the next arrivals, similar to, and possibly related to, them in nearly every known particular. These are, of course, the doughty Firbolgs who seem to have taken over the country from the Fomorians without any difficulty. This is of some importance as we'll see in a minute, and again points to the fact that the other invaders were alien to both Fomorian and Firbolg alike.

The next to arrive were the Tuatha de Danaan, the magicians from the east. (P. W. Joyce, by the way, states categorically that the Tuatha de Danaan 'spent some time in Greece where they learned magic and other curious arts.' It is far more likely that their magic hailed from their own traditions and way of life in Scythia and among the Perisans.) They surpassed, according to the Leabhar Gabhala, the sages of the arts of heathendom (*sic*) in learning lore and magic and druidism and cunning. They learned their arts in four cities – Falias, Gorias, Murias and Findias – which I have not been able to identify, but which have the singular Persian S-ending in common, which was applied only to persons or places of uncommon attributes. Out of Falias came the stone of Fal (Liath Fail) which was at Tara, and on which the kings of Ireland were crowned. Out of Gorias came the spear of Lugh Lamh Fada (the spear thrower?). Out of Findias was brought the sword of Nuada, another Danaan hero, and out of Murias came the Dagda's cauldron, from which no one ever went hungry. The Dagda was a great warrior king of the Danaan, who is said to have reigned from a.m. 3370 to 3450.

The de Danaans defeated the Firbolgs at the two battles of Moytura, a place near Cong in County Mayo. The first of these battles, which according to Joyce lasted four days, was fought a.m. 3303, and the Firbolgs were defeated with great slaughter and their king killed. Afterwards the de Danaans took possession of the country, but, with characteristic improvidence for the future, allowed a powerful nation of Firbolgs to live in Connacht. A thing which was nearly their undoing for, some 27 years later, in a.m. 3330 – on the eve of Samhain, or October 31st according to Joyce – the second battle of Moytura took place.

Now Nuada of the Silver Hand, who was, according to the Four Masters King of Ireland from a.m. 3311 to 3330, lost his hand during the first battle of Moytura during which he commanded the de Danaans. A new arm was made for him by the great de Danaan artificer Creidne and attached to his stump by the great physician Dianecht, but the cure took seven years (3303 – 3311) during which time Bres, like Lugh, of mixed blood, half de Danaan and half Fomorian ruled Ireland as regent. At the end of seven years, however, he had to retire in favour of Nuada. Whereupon he promptly went to the land of the Fomorians, variously given as Lochlann (Scandinavia) and Alba (Scotland), instigated an invasion of Ireland with a Fomorian army which would be aided by the disaffected Firbolgs, and which was to be commanded by the Fomorian, Balor of the Evil Eye. During the battle Balor killed Nuada, but was himself slain by Lugh with his far-reaching weapon.

The entire story surrounding these battles, the motives, the actions and the outcomes, is typically Hellenic in structure, for it begins with a dream in which Balor was warned that his grandson would kill him; he thereupon had Lugh sent to be drowned when he was born, but Lugh survived through the kindness of those given the task of his destruction, to fulfill the prophesy that he would kill his grandfather. It is very reminiscent of the story of Astyages, the Median king, who tried to kill the young Cyrus in much the same way, and with similar results.

The battle in which the Milesians are said to have defeated the de Danaan's decisively was the Battle of Taillteann, in Meath.

The Lydians, a contiguous people to the Ionians on the Asia Minor coast and who intermarried and formed alliances with them, were also an Hellenic people, living in what had been Scythian dominated territory, as seafarers and colonists. They were the first known people to use gold and silver coinage and introduce retail trade (and let it be noted that many authorities hold that it was the search for gold that brought these Mediterranean settlers across the world to Ireland in the first place.) They also claimed to have invented the games popularly played all over Attica and reaching their climax during the Olympic games at Corinth. The story goes that the games were invented at the time they first sent a colony to Tyrrhenia during the reign of Atys, son of Manes. During this time Lydia suffered a famine and, to alleviate the suffering somewhat, they invented games which they would play all day on alternate days, and eat on the days in between. After eighteen years when there was no improvement in their famine condition, the king decided to divide the population into two lots one of which should emigrate and the other remain at home. Those who sailed away were commanded by the king's son, Tyrrhenus, and they sailed until they came to northern Italy where they settled changing their name when they landed to Tyrrhenians and calling their country Tyrrhenia – which area some authorities have claimed as the sole birthplace of the Irish Milesians. This, however, is clearly wrong. But it is undoubtedly the colony of their friends and neighbours in Asia Minor, the Lydians, who were so fond of games.

Now it is a traditional fact that Lugh, son of a de Danaan father and a Firbolg mother, instituted at Taillteann a series of games on the Olympic model *inhonour of his foster-mother,* Taillte, who was, of course, a de Danaan.

It is conceivable that the defeat of the de Danaan at Taill-teann by the Milisians was not a military defeat, but a blood-less victory on the sportsfield, which would be more in accord with the veneration and awe in which the Milesians sub-sequently held their de Danaan forerunners because of their magic rites and practices. It may be too conjectural. It may be that the Battle of Taillteann, the home of the games, was a bloody affair; but it is a reevant factor in this hypothesis that these games were initiated on the Lydian pattern by a leader whose people might very well have hailed from a Lydian settlement.

In explanation of the origin of Lugh and Nuada, it was accepted practice, particularly by the Lydians and Milesians, to breed with the women of the people they conquered.

Now, according to M. A. Hutton, who devoted considerable time and study to the Celtic mythologies towards the end of the last century, the version of Cuchullain's training found in the *Foghlaimh Conchulaind,* an unedited tract at the time, gives in detail the story of his training which is presupposed in the versions contained in the *Leabhar na h-Uidri* and in the *Book of Leinster,* the accepted sources of the Tain Bo Cuail-gne. In this work Cuchullain is trained by Scatha, the warrior-queen-teacher, in Scythia and in Great Greece. The name Scythia, she adds, occurs frequently in old Irish literature, Scythia being 'a vague term for a region extending from what is now Hungary, eastward far into Asia.' In other words in what was utterly Celtic country. That there should have been frequent intercourse between the Celts of Ireland and the Celts of Europe, and that young Irish nobles should have gone from Ireland to get warlike training among the Celts of the Continent, seems only what one might expect. In Kuno Meyer's edited version of the Wooing of Emer by Cuchullain one finds that Cuchullain went to Scatha, *'fri Alpi allaanoir',* 'eastward from the Alpi'. This has been argued, rather carelessly, as meaning that he went to Albyn, in fact to the Isle of Skye, and that it was there that Scatha had her warlike school. But eastward from Alpi would not answer the position of Skye relative to Scotland; but it would very well answer the position of Scythia relative to the Alps. Furthermore, the Book of Leinster refers to Cuchullain's training in Armenia and to his wars with – significantly, perhaps in the light of the fact that his teacher was also a woman – the *Cichloiste,* or Amazons. There appears to be no reason why Amazons should otherwise find themselves in an Irish legend than that they came into contact with its hero.

And there is one final point worthy of mention which is that the religion of the early Irish was neither pantheistic like that of later European neighbours, nor anthropomorphic like that of the Greeks, but was similar to that of the Asiatic Milesians and the Lydians, which was a rather harmonious and sophisticated blend of the two:.. so far as any information is available on the subject at all. This, of course, would also help to explain the ease with which Christianity established itself in Ireland in the fifth century.

Here, now, is an anonymous poem written apparently about the beginning of the last century by an itinerant Irish versifier. It is called The Invaders of Ireland:

> Should any inquire about Erin
> It is I who can give him the truth
> Concerning the deeds of each daring
> Invader, since time was a youth.
>
> First Cassir, Bith's ventursome daughter,
> Came here o'er the eastern sea;
> And fifty fair damsels she brought her
> To solace her warriors three.
>
> Bith died at the foot of his mountain,
> And Ladr on top of his height;
> And Cassir by Boyle's limpid fountain,
> Ere rushed down the flood in its might.
>
> For a year, while the waters encumber
> The Earth, at Tul-tunna of strength,
> I slept, none enjoyed such sweet slumber,
> As that which I woke from at length.

When Partholon came to the Island
From Greece, in the Eastern land,
I welcomed him gaily to my land,
And feasted the whole of his band.

Again, when death seized on the strangers
I roamed the land merry and free,
Both careless and fearless of dangers,
Till blithe Nemed came over the sea.

The Firbolgs and roving Firgallions
Came next like the waves in their flow;
The Firdonnians arrived in Battalions
and landed in Erris – Mayo.

Then came the wise Tuatha de Danaans,
Concealed in black clouds from their foe;
I feasted with them near the Shannon,
Though that was a long time ago.

After them came the children of Mile
From Spain, o'er the southern waves;
I lived with the tribes as their file
And chanted the deeds of their braves.

Time ne'er my existence could wither,
From death's grasp I always was freed,
Till Patrick the Christian came hither
To spread the Redeemer's pure creed.

Perhaps the most significant thing about the Irish myths
for the student of letters is that they were written when the
literatures of modern Europe had not yet been born and the
literary en gies of the ancient world were dead. These Irish
legends are the connecting link between the two and were
first written down in early Christian Ireland, which had not
felt the direct influence of Rome, among a people for
whom the tales were still vivid and who, perhaps, inherited a
rudimentary literature drawn from ancient Celtic sources. At
all events, now began to emerge men who, because of their
work on these tales, became the earliest classical scholars in

the modern world.

It is maintained by a number of authorities that the influence of the literary works familiar to the Irish emigrant scholars of the sixth to the tenth centuries bore a singular influence on the development of the literatures of France, Germany and Italy. The form of the twelfth century French romance 'Aucassin and Nicolette', according to A. H. Leahy, is that of the chief Irish romances and may, he maintains, have been suggested by them.

'It is as hard,' he writes, 'to suppose that the beautiful literature of Ireland had absolutely no influence upon nations known to be in contact with it, as it would be to hold the belief that the ancient Cretan civilisation had no effect upon the literary development that culminated in the poems of Homer.'

We have already considered the question of the possibility of these myths containing a germ of truth, therefore it is pointless to waste time arguing against the frequently heard theory that the legends and stories are inaccurate survivals of pre-Christian works, added to by successive generations of bards. It makes little difference to my foregoing argument whether this was so or not, but in addition to any intrinsic fact that they may contain, the stories have a literary merit of their own, a style and character of their own, which would, surely, have been lost and dissipated in the process of constant mutation of the order implied by those who maintain that they have grown solely from the minds of bards. Furthermore, the sophistication of the tales, like the sophistication of the great tales of Greece, is that of art brought to bear on ideas, however bald and ancient the idea itself.

To take a classical illustration, which Healy used in a similar context, the barbarity shown by Aeneas in Aeneid X, in sacrificing four young men on the funeral pyre of Pallas was an act which, if it occurred in Virgil's day, would have caused utter horror. Nor does it prove that there was an ancient tale of Pallas in which victims were sacrificed like that, nor even that such victims were sacrificed in Latium at that time.

But it does suggest that Virgil was familiar with the idea of such sacrifices, and his sense of drama impelled him to use it in the Pallas episode, for he would hardly have invented it.

Thus, as already emphasised in the man in the bar, the artifact may itself be polished to a fine glow, but the grain of truth within remains.

The tales given below are chosen for several reasons, but principally because they represent all that is best and different in the myths of Ireland.

The first, and one of the oldest, is set in the earliest period, that closest to the Hellenic fatherland, it may be, and is one of the Three Great Tragedies of the Gael, *The Fate of the Children of Tuireann*. It's similarity to the story of Jason and the Argonauts is too obvious to need much comment. The other two tragedies of the Gael are, of course, *The Children of Lir*, and *Deirdre and the Sons of Usna* which is, and must remain, one of the finest stories of its kind in the world. [1]

It is as great and as moving in concept, both of incident and of character, as the Iliad; the story is fast moving and is told with a great deal of deliberate art, for example in the restraint shown in the tragic death of Deirdre and in the remarkable and well-sustained lament of hers before she is killed.

The Wooing of Etain, with its strong supernatural flavour, its observation of nature and its insistence on the idea of regeneration, its mystical quality, is an important story. [2]

And finally *The Combat at the Ford*, perhaps the finest example of the genre that has survived to us.

Eoin Neeson
Dublin, 1965

1. See *The Second Book of Irish Myths and Legends* by the same author — forthcoming Mercier paperback.
2. There are two versions of this legend, the details of both being combined in the one given here.

The Fate of the Children of Tuireann

CHAPTER ONE

At the first great battle of Moytura the Tuatha de Danaan routed and killed great multitudes of Firbolgs in four bloody days, driving the remainder west into Connacht — so-called because of a great king and magician there called Conn, who showed his power by covering the province one day with snow, so that ever after it was called Conn-sneachta or Conn's snow. And the de Danaan were happy enough with this arrangement, because they had suffered enough in the battle themselves, and not the least of their hardships and tribulations was the fact that their King, Nuada, has his right arm cut off at the shoulder by a hairy Firbolg champion called Sreng. And after that he was in great pain and torment and nearly died. But Diancecht, the great de Danaan physician, healed the stump and made for Nuada an arm of silver which he set in its place, so that the king forever afterwards was called Nuada of the Silver Hand. And still and all he was sick and troubled with his arm and unfit for the cares of the kingdom of Eire, so that he made Bres regent for him in the interim.

But Bres was only half a de Danaan, and that on his mother's side. For his father was Balor, king of the Fomorians. And while it might have been good politics to give the regency to Bres had Bres been an honourable man, Bres was not an *honourable man*. He laid the race of the de Danaan under a tribute to his father's people, and exacted it with great severity. And all this time Nuada was in great pain and suffering and was unable to help his people.

Then one day Nuada's steward, who was a one eyed man — having lost the other in the same battle in which his king lost an arm — was standing in the sun on the ramparts of Royal Tara looking across the golden and the green plain around it with his one eye, when he saw approaching the

25

palace two fine looking young men who greeted him as they came closer. The steward returned the greeting.

'Who are ye,' he asked, 'and where might ye be from?'

'We are Miach and Omiach,' they replied, 'sons of Diancecht and good physicians ourselves.'

'Well, if ye are,' said the steward, 'maybe ye could put an eye back where my own eye used to be.'

'I could put,' said one of them, 'the eye of that cat in your lap where your eye was.'

'Fair enough,' said the steward, and without more ado it was done. But it was a mixed blessing for the steward, although he was delighted at the time, for as sure as he wanted to rest or to sleep, the eye would leap at the squeek of a mouse; at the flight of a bird or a rustling in the reeds; and when he wanted to look at a banquet or a great assembly of warriors, that is the very time it chose to close and go to sleep.

But none of this worried him at the time he got it and he ran forthwith in to Nuada and told him that great physicians had come to Tara: 'For,' he said, 'they have put the eye of a cat into the place of my own eye.'

'Bring them in,' said Nuada.

Now, as Miach and Omiach entered the palace, they heard a great and pitiful sigh.

'That is the sigh of a warrior,' said Miach.

'It could be the sigh of a warrior with a daol, blackening him on one side,' said Omiach.

Now it should be explained that a daol, or darbh-daol, is not a good thing to have with you; for it is a thing in the form of a chafer or cockchafer, like a beetle or cockroach; but a daol will fasten on a man, or a woman for that matter, and suck the life and the goodness out of him. So it was that Omiach said what he said.

The king was brought to the physicians, the sons of the Diancecht who made the silver arm for him, and they examined him. They drew out the arm from his side and out of it there bounded a daol through the palace, and the whole household followed it and killed it.

Then Miach searched for an arm of equal length and thickness as his own to give the king, but among all the Tuatha de Danaan not an arm could be found that would

26

suit him except that of Modhan the swineherd. This the king could not have, of course, because of what Modhan was.

'Would the bones of the king's own arm suit you,' Miach was asked.

'That is what we would prefer,' he replied.

And so a man was sent for the arm to the battlefield of Moytura and he brought it with him to Tara and the dis-interred arm was given to Miach.

Then Miach said to Omiach: 'Would you prefer to set the arm or to go for the herbs that will put flesh on it when 'tis set?'

And Omiach replied: 'I would prefer to set the arm.'

So Miach went for the herbs and brought them back, and than the arm was set and clothed with new flesh by them.

Now, although it is not properly part of this story, it is no harm to know the result of this. Because Miach was a better doctor than his father Diancecht, and subsituted for the silver arm a real one of flesh and bone, set joint to joint and sinew to sinew and clothed in flesh in 'three moments', his father Diancecht was so enraged at this damaging competition that he took a sword, when he learned of what Miach had done, and slew him. Where he buried the body, however, there grew, up through the soil of the grave, three hundred and sixty five healing herbs, one for every sinew and joint of the young physicians's body — each herb to cure a disease in that part of the body from which it grew. These were plucked and gathered in their proper order into her cloak by Miach's sister Airmed, also more skilled than Diancecht; but he, when he heard of it and with his anger still unappeased, came and mixed them all on her so that their separate and great virtues were lost forever.

Now, sometime after these events and yet before the Second battle of Moytura, Nuada and the principal people of the Tuatha de Danaan were assembled at the Hill of Uisneach, one of the Royal residences, for a bitter purpose. And that was to pay the annual taxes to the Fomorians that Bres had imposed upon them. This tax was a tax upon each kneading trough, a tax upon the quern or grindstone, a tax on the baking flags and an ounce of gold for each person of the Tuatha de Danaan who could be stood upon the Hill of Uisneach. If this tax, equally hard upon a man's pocket and on his stomach, was not paid, then the man who refused had his nose cut off by the Fomorian tyrants.

Now, as Nuada and his chieftains stood waiting uneasily on the Hill of Uisneach for the Fomorian tax-gatherers, across the plain towards them they saw coming from the east a band of armed men led by a young man of great command and, as they say, with a radiance about him like the sunset. They were Lugh Lamh Fada and his foster-brothers, the Clan Mananaan – the sons of Mananaan Mac Lir whose real name was Oirbsen the Navigator and who lived at Emain Abhlach, the Palace of the Apple Trees and which is now known as the Isle of Arran in the Firth of Clyde. And Lugh, the Il-Dana or man of sciences, was the son of Cian and a grandson of Balor, but he had no love for his grandfather's people who oppressed the de Danaan.

And not alone was Lugh a man of great science and knowledge; a man of proud and noble bearing, but he was equipped as such a man should be. The horse he rode was Mananaan's Aonvarr, as swift as the winds of spring and equally so whether she raced over land or sea. And, so 'tis said, no rider could be killed from her back. He wore Mananaan's armour which protected him well, for he could not be wounded under it, over it or throught it; and across his breast he had the torque of Mananaan, which no weapon could pierce. He wore a jewelled helmet to protect his head, and when he took it off his eager face was a bright as a sun-filled summer's day. At his left side hung the Freagra, the Answerer, the sword of Mananaan, from whose wound no one could survive and which, when it was drawn from its scabbard, melted the strength of hostile warriors, when they saw it, to that of women.

And so, led by this mighty leader, these troops from the east rode to where Nuada and his people stood on the Hill who welcomed them. But hardly were the friendly greetings over when they all saw coming towards them another group of armed men, but different to the first in every way. They were a heavily armed band of eighty-one surly and evil-looking men on whom was marked the stamp of cruelty, and they were the Fomorian tax-gatherers, led by Eine, Eithfath, Coron and Cokpar who had the reputation of being the cruellest and fiercest of them all. When Nuada and his people saw them coming each one of them stood up before them, much to the surprise of Lugh, who asked:

'Why do you stand for these savages when you didn't stand for us?'

'Because,' said Nuada, 'we dare not do otherwise, for if there was one of us, even a child a month old, who stayed sitting in their presence, that would be excuse enough for them to kill us all.'

Lugh said nothing for a moment. Then:

'By God,' he said, 'they should be killed themselves.'

For another moment he stayed silent, and still the king and all his people remained standing before the Fomorians.

'By God,' said Lugh then, 'I'll kill them myself.'

'And if you do,' said the king, 'it will only do more harm than good, for the Fomorians would bring an army and destroy us completely.'

But Lugh ignored him crying:

'This oppression has gone on long enough,' and with that he drew the Answerer and attacked the Fomorians until all but nine of them were dead, and they escaped only because they ran, while Lugh was slaughtering their comrades, to Nuada and put themselves under his protection against the rage of Lugh.

Then Lugh turned to them:

'I would kill you also,' he said, 'but I'm sparing you so that you can go back and tell your foreign king what you have seen.'

So the nine tax-gatherers returned across the sea to Lochlann, or Scandinavia, where the Fomorians were and told them what had happened, that the only reason Lugh had spared them was that they might tell it to their king, Balor.

When he had heard everything, Balor turned to his chiefs and said: 'Who is he?'

But they did not know who he was until Caitlin, Balor's queen, said: 'I know who he is; he is the Il-dana, our grandson, our own daughter's son. And it is prophesied that when he comes to Eire our power there will end.'

But Balor did not believe her because he had also heard this prophesy and had taken steps to avoid it. For it had also been prophesied that Balor would be killed by his grandson. So, when his daughter, Ethlenn, who had married the de Danaan nobleman Cian, was pregnant he made his plans. When the child was born and turned out to be a boy, Balor had the infant taken away. He gave it to one of his retainers, who lived by the sea, with instructions to see that the child was drowned. But because he did not say why, the infant survived and this is how he did so. The wife of the retainer was also pregnant, and gave birth to a still born child just at that time. She was so distressed that the retainer, seeing no harm in it, substituted the living infant for the dead one, which he disposed of in the sea. Lugh survived and eventually came under the patronage of Mananaan, who recognised him for what he was.

But all this Balor did not know. Therefore he did not believe his wife, who was a sorceress among the Fomorians, when she told him that this hero was the Il-Dana.

So Balor and his chiefs, Caitlin and the druids and poets and philosophers of the Fomorians, and Balor's twelve sons went into council. After they had discussed the situation for a while, Bress, whose authority it was that had been flouted in Eire by Lugh and the de Danaan, stood up and said: 'I'll take an army of seven great brigades of horsemen of the Fomorian army and find this Il-Dana and destroy him, and I'll bring his head to you at our palace of Berva in Eire.'

This proposal was agreed to by Balor and the Fomorian chiefs, and they began to make detailed plans.

Warships and transports were prepared for Bres and his men; their seams were freshly caulked with pitch and they were loaded with provisions and weapons. Meanwhile Luath the Long and Lugh the Storyteller were sent throughout Lochlann to summon the cavalry soldiers that Bres wanted. When they were all assembled they checked their weapons and equipment and sailed for Eire.

Balor stood beside the ships in the harbour before they sailed and said: 'Find the Il-Dana and destroy him and cut off his head. And when you have that done, make fast your cables to the island of Eire, which gives us nothing but trouble, and tow it far to the north of Lochlann letting the great ocean fill its place. Leave it there in the cold north where none of the Tuatha de Danaan will ever follow it.

Then, with blazing sails filling the sky over them, and with one, concerted stroke, the newly rigged fleet moved out from the harbour upon the moving sea, over the mighty sea and the awful and cold abyss, mounting the ridges of the waves and the treacherous mountains of the bottomless ocean until they made harbour in Eas-Dara, or Ballysodare as it is now, in Sligo. And they were quick to disembark and let their fury loose on the western part of Connacht, which they devastated.

Now the king of that part of Eire, where the Fomorians were aided by their kinsmen and allies, the Firbolgs, was the Bodbh Dearg, son of the Dagda More, or Great Dagda, Eochaid Ollav, mighty king and oracle of the Tuatha de Danaan, whose palace was at the Boyne, near Tara.

The Bodbh Dearg immediately sent to Tara for help from Lugh, who was still there with Nuada because Lugh had routed and slain a pocket of Fomorians in Eas Dara while the Fomorians had been planning the invasion. It was dawn when the news reached him, with the spearpoint of day striking at the night, and he immediately prepared Aonvarr of the Flowing Mane. Then he went and asked Nuada for his help.

'I'll meet them,' said Lugh, 'as quickly as I can, but I need more men. I'd like to ask you for them so that they may come with me now.'

But Nuada refused. 'I will not give my men,' he said, 'to avenge a deed that has not been done against myself.'

Lugh, when he heard this, could hardly contain his anger and, turning on his heel, he strode from the king's presence and mounting his steed, rode westward from Tara.

CHAPTER TWO

Lugh hadn't gone very far when he saw three fully armed warriors riding towards him. When he got closer he recognised them as his father, Cian, and his two uncles Cu and Cethan, the sons of his grandfather, Cainte. He greeted them and they asked him:

'What has you up so early?'

'Trouble enough,' said Lugh, 'for the Fomorians have landed and are destroying Bodbh Dearg, the Dagda's son. I'm on my way to help him and give them battle and I'm wondering what help I can expect from you?'

'We're with you,' they said, 'and there's not a man of us but will keep a hundred Fomorians from you in the battle.'

'Good enough,' said Lugh, 'but there is something else I'd prefer you to do first, and that is to ride through the country and summon the warriors of the Sidhe, the spirit world, to me from wherever they are.'

And with that they separated. Cu and Cethan went southward, Lugh continued his journey to the west, and Cian, Lugh's father made his way northward through the plain of Muirthemne, which is in the centre of Eire.

And it is at this point that our story proper begins, for Cian had not gone very far when he, in his turn, saw three fully armed warriors coming towards him and he recognised them as three de Danaan chiefs, the sons of Tuireann, Brian, Uar and Uraca. Now it so happend that there was a fued of great bitterness between the three sons of Cainte — that is Cian and his brothers who had gone south to rouse the Spirit army for Lugh — and the sons of Tuireann, so much so that, if they chanced to meet, it was a foregone conclusion that none would survive the encounter but the stronger party.

No sooner did Cian see the three sons of Tuireann than he said to himself:

'Now if only Cu and Cethan were here it would be a wonderful fight; but since they are not, and I am only one against three, I would be well advised to fly.'

Near him was a herd of swine rooting in the rich soil of Muirthemne and Cian promptly changed himself into the appearance of one of them with a druidical wand, and joined the herd, rooting at the soil like the others.

But he had no sooner done so than Brian, eldest of the Sons of Tuireann, said:

'Brothers, did ye see a warrior crossing the plain a moment ago?'

'We did,' they replied.

'And where has he gone?' asked Brian.

'Damned if we know,' they replied, and Brian admonished them for their carelessness.

'It is foolish and careless of you,' he said, 'not to be more alert in open country in time of war. Now I know what has happened to him; he has changed himself, with a druid's ·

wand, into the shape of a pig and is now rooting with that herd there. And you can take it,' he added, 'that whatever else he is, he is no friend of ours, for if he was why would he do it?'

'That's bad enough,' said Uar and Uraca, 'but what's worse is that you know as well as we do that the man who owns that herd would have the three of us killed if we hurt any of his pigs, and how are we to know our enemy unless we kill them all?'

'Ye're a bright pair,' said Brian, 'when for all your schooling you can't distinguish a druidical pig from a real one, and if you'd paid attention to what you were being taught you could. But I can,' he said, and as he said it he touched his two brothers with a druidical wand of his own and turned them into a pair of fleet, slender, eager hounds which straightaway put their keen noses to the scent and made for the herd giving tongue ravenously.

When they came near the herd, Cian, still in the shape of the pig, made a break for a nearby wood where he sought to find shelter, but Brian who had cut across his path hurled is spear through his chest.

Immediately the pig screamed out in a human voice:

'Why did you do this evil, knowing who I am?'

'Your voice,' said Brian, 'is the voice of a man, but your shape is the shape of a pig, and I do not know you by either your voice or your shape.'

And the pig answered: 'I am Cian, son of Cainte, and I ask quarter.'

To this Uar and Uraca, who had resumed their human forms and joined them, said: 'Indeed we will grant it, and we regret what has happened.'

But Brian said: 'Indeed, and I swear it by the gods of the sky, if you had seven lives I would take them all.'

'Well,' said Cian, 'if you would, you would. But grant me one last request.'

'What is it?' asked Brian.

'Allow me to resume my proper form before you kill me,' said Cian.

'Very well,' said Brian, 'for,' he added, fiercely, 'in some cases I think less of killing the man than the pig.'

Cian accordingly took his own shape and said:

33

'Will you grant me quarter now?'

'We will not,' answered Brian.

'Indeed,' he said, 'ye are the sons of Tuireann, and are about to kill me; but even so I have circumvented ye, for had I been killed as a pig, there would only have been due on me the eric of a pig, but now that I am a man again you will pay the eric of a man. And moreover,' he said, 'never was there killed and never shall there be killed a man for whom a greater fine shall be paid than you will have to pay for me, for even the weapons with which I am killed will cry abroad the killing to my son.'

'In that case,' said Brian, 'it is not with weapons that you will be killed, but with the stones of the earth.' And with that he and his brothers threw aside their arms and, seizing the boulders that lay scattered about, hurled them at the wretched Cian with hatred and violence, until he was reduced to a frightful and disfigured mass. Then they dug a grave six feet deep and buried him. But the very earth itself, angry at this fratricide — for the sons of Cainte and the sons of Tuireann were blood relatives — refused the body from them and cast it back again to the surface. And six times the sons of Tuireann buried the battered body of their kinsman Cian in the earth, and six times the earth refused it; but on the seventh time the earth refused no longer and the body remained where it was buried. Then the sons of Tuireann, who had been on their way to join Lugh in battle with the Fomorians, took up their arms again and prepared to resume their journey. But as they did so from the very soil beneath their feet, they thought they heard a voice, faint and muffled crying:

'The blood upon your hands, Oh sons of Tuireann,
Will there remain until we meet again.'

Meanwhile Lught had continued westward through Athlone and Roscommon and over Moylurg and the Curlew Mountains until he reached the great plain where the Fomorians had their camp, filled now with their plunder of Connacht.

As he approached Bres stood up and looked towards where Lugh, who had circled the camp, was coming through the night.

'There,' said Bres, 'is a strange and remarkable thing, for the sun, that rises every other day in the east is rising now out of the west.'

'And better for us, perhaps,' said his druids, 'that it should stay where it ought to be.'

'What else could it be but the sun?' asked Bres.

'The light you see,' said the druids, 'is the flashing of his weapons and the radiance of the Il Dana himself; the man whose head you seek, who killed our tax-collectors and is now on his way here.'

And shortly afterwards, true enough, Lugh came up and greeeted them.

'What are you doing here,' they said, 'since you are, as we know well, our enemy.'

'And why wouldn't I be here,' asked Lugh who knew what he was about, 'for isn't only one half of me de Danaan, while the other half is from you; am I not the son of the daughter of Balor himself? And now I come in peace to ask you for the milch cows you have taken from the people of Connacht.'

And then, an angry and bad-tempered Fomorian chief, shouted: 'May the light of day abandon you until you get a single one of them.'

And all the others shouted at Lugh in much the same strain.

But Lugh, who was the Il-Dana or man of science, cast a spell upon the cattle so that the milch cows were returned to their owners and the dry cows were left behind to encumber the Fomorians and tie them to their camp until the warriors Lugh had sent for arrived to give them battle.

For three days and three nights Lugh harried the Fomorians until the army he had sent for arrived. Shortly afterwards Bodbh Dearg arrived also, bringing with him an army of three thousand men.

'What's the delay,' he shouted to Lugh as he rode up on his sweating horse, the sun glinting from his armour.

'Waiting for you,' shouted Lugh back at him with a grin, and with that he sprang to arm himself with the arms and armour he wore when he first saw Nuada of the Silver Hand on the Hill of Uisneach. In addition he slung about him a great, dark-blue shield and his two, heavy socketed, thick-handled, deadly spears that were said to have been tempered in the blood of poisonous snakes. Then the entire army, kings, heroes and warriors, made a battle phalanx; before and above them they raised a bulwark of glittering spears protruding through their locked shields as they advanced.

The Fomorians were ready and, when the advancing phalanx of the men of Eire was within range, they hurled flight after flight of javelins so that the air became thick with them, like flights of birds homing in the evening, and the same rush was in the air with their passage; and underneath the screams of wounded men and blood where they fell on the saturated ground. But still the phalanx advanced on the Fomorian camp, and now it was the great, broad-bladed spears that did their deadly work, and the clash and the noise were awful; and when the spears broke and were lost in the bodies of men, then they drew their wide grooved, golden crossed swords and fought foot to foot and shield to shield; and over them and above them rose forests of leaping flame from the din and the wrath of battle.

Then Lugh, standing in the middle of the great carnage, looked around him for the battle-pen, or headquarters of Bres, from which he would direct the battle. Standing there, tall among the blood-mad warriors, Lugh sought through the smoke and the confusion for Bres. Across the writhing bodies of men pinned to the ground with broken spear shafts, the piled corpses of men who fell by the sword, the naked and headless bodies of those who had already been stripped of their armour. He searched until he saw the battle-pen of Bres. And than he rushed towards it in so great a fury that a countless number of Fomorians fell before him until he drove himself right to the son of Balor whose bodyguard now lay dead around him.

But even as Lugh prepared to kill Bres, the other appealed to him, saying: 'Don't kill me, Lugh. We are, after all, related, so let there be peace between us, since nothing can withstand your blows. Let there be peace now and I will undertake, by the sun and the moon, by the sea and the land and by all the elements, to bring my Fomorians to your assistance at Moytura where you will surely face my father, Balor of the Evil Eye, provided they do not desert me.'

Then, when the Fomorians saw their chieftain captured by Lugh, they too dropped their arms and asked for peace; and next the druids of the Fomorians and their men of learning came to Lugh and asked him to spare their lives, and Lugh answered them:

'So far from wanting to kill you,' he said, 'I swear that had the whole Fomorian tribe gone under your protection, I would have spared them.'

And, after they had acknowledged Lugh and returned their spoils, Bres and what remained of his army returned to Lochlann with their druids.

CHAPTER THREE

When the day was over and the last of the Fomorians had gone from the field, Lugh saw two of his kinsmen among the host of exhausted warriors, resting now after the battle. He asked them if they had seen his father, Cian, anywhere. 'We did not,' they said.

'Was he killed by the Fomorians?' Asked Lugh.

'He was not,' they replied, 'for there was no sign of him in the battle.'

'Then,' said Lugh, 'he is dead, for if he was alive nothing would have prevented him from coming. I know he's dead,' he went on, 'and until I know how he died and who killed him neither food nor drink will pass my lips.'

Then, with a small band of companions, he retraced the way he had come until he reached the place where he had parted from his father a few days previously. From there he travelled north to the plain of Muirthemne where Cian was forced to turn himself into the shape of a pig when he saw the sons of Tuireann.

And when Lugh reached this place, he stopped and dismounted and walked across the earth without knowing why he did so. And as he walked the very stones of the earth beneath his feet spoke with a single voice and said:

'Here lies the body of your father Cian, Lugh, forced to take the shape of a pig when he saw the three sons of Tuireann; but killed by them in his own form; the blood upon the hands of the Tuireann, there will remain till they meet Cian again.'

Lugh listened to these words silently. Then, calling his own people to him, he went directly to the spot where the sons of Tuireann had buried his father and disinterred the body so that they might see how the murder was committed. When they saw it, and the dreadful condition it was in, Lugh remained silent for a long while.

Then, giving his father three kisses, he said: 'A cruel and vicious murder have the sons of Tuireann given to my father. My God, I am sick to think of it. I can't see, or hear or feel in my heart for grief. Oh God, why wasn't I here? Oh God, Oh God that's bad enough, but that a de Danaan should kill another and a relative. I swear to you that because of this fratricide, the curse of brother against brother will be the curse of Eire for countless generations.'

And having made this prophesy, he made the following lament above the body of his father:

'Frightful only can be called the evil done to Cian
The mangling of whose body has crippled my own;
And eastward by all her roads
And westward by all her soil
For a great while will Eire be filled with evil.

The death of Cian, the great champion,
Has left me like a walking corpse,
Without strength, without power, without a feeling of life.
The Tuireann have killed him and I say,
With the knowledge of my hatred,
It will came against them and theirs to the ends of the
world.'

Then, when Cian was buried again and a monument with his name engraved on it erected above him, Lugh said:

'This hill here on which he died will be called after Cian from this on. Now, let us go back to Tara where Nuada sits with the de Danaan chiefs around him. But say nothing of all this until I myself have mentioned it first.'

So they returned to Tara, Lugh following them. And when he reached there he was received with great honour and ceremony, being put to sit at the right hand of the king, for news of his great success over the Fomorians had long preceded him to Tara where they were already celebrating the victory when he arrived.

Lugh said nothing as he sat down and appeared calm and composed. But he looked about the great hall until he saw the sons of Tuireann among the throng. And it was clear who they were and what they were, for in all things they excelled any of the champions there assembled. In fleetness of foot there was none to compare with them; in feats of arms the same, and in addition they were by far the handsomest. And only Lugh himself had surpassed their deeds and courage in the battle with the Fomorians. Therefore the king had honoured them too above anyone except Lugh. Then Lugh asked that the gong of silence be rung, and when it was struck and the notes had died away and with them the hum and clatter of conversation and all were listening, he said:

'Men of the Tuatha de Danaan, now that I have your attention, I wish only to ask one queston. It is this; what vengeance would each of you take on those who knowingly killed your father?'

For a moment there was a stunned slence; and then Nuada said:

'What do you mean. Surely it is not your father, Cian, who has been killed?'

'I regret,' said Lugh, 'to tell you that it is indeed my father who has been killed and here, in this hall, I see those who slew him, and they know better than I the manner in which they did it.'

The sons of Tuireann said nothing; but Nuada jumping to his feet said:

'Not one day, or two days, would it take the man who killed my father to die; but as many days as it would take him if I lopped off a member from his body each day until he cried for death from the torment under my hands.'

At this there was a great shout of acclamation and angry agreement from those present, in which the sons of Tuireann joined like the rest. And Lugh, who had been watching them closely, said, when the clamour had died down:

'The murderers here have passed judgement upon themselves, for they joined with the rest of you in your agreement. And as you are here to bear witness, men of the de

Danaan, I claim the right to put an eric on them for my father. If they refuse it, I will not violate the sanctuary of the king's palace, but, by God, they will not leave this hall without settling accounts with me at the doorway.'

Then Nuada said: 'If it was I had killed your father, Lugh, I would be well satisfied if you were willing to accept an eric fine from me.'

Then the sons of Tuireann whispered among themselves; 'He's talking for our benefit,' said Uar and Uraca, 'it's obvious that he knows it all, however he does, and it seems better that we should confess now rather than try to hide it and have him condemn us.'

Brian, however, had his doubts.

'Maybe he's only trying to get a confession out of us,' he said, 'because he's not sure, and then he would not accept the eric fine when he knows for sure.'

But Uar and Uraca persisted and said: 'It is your right to confess, since you are the eldest,' they said, 'but if you don't we'll do it ourselves.'

Then Brian stood up at his place and said:

'What you are saying is directed at us, Lugh, because it is well known that there is enmity between your father and his brothers and us, and if one of them is dead, who is most likely to have killed him in your opinion, but ourselves. Yet Cian was not killed by any weapons of the sons of Tuireann. But, because of what I said, we therefore will give an eric to you as if it was so.'

'Very well,' said Lugh, 'and I will accept an eric from you, even though you doubt my word on this, and I will say here and now what it is, and if you think any part of it is too great, then I am willing to remit that part of it.'

'That seems fair enough to us,' said Brian, 'what is the eric?'

Then, looking closely at them, Lugh said:

'Here it is; first, three apples; second, the skin of a pig; third, a spear; fourth, two horses and a chariot; fifth, seven pigs; sixth, a hound-pup; seventh a cooking spit and eighth, three shouts on a hill.'

The assembly had been looking at him in astonishment as he said this, and it was easy to see the look of relief and perplexity mingled that stood out on the faces of the sons of

Tuireann. Uar and Uraca were visibly relieved, but only Brian frowned in doubt.

'Now,' said Lugh, 'that is the eric I ask from you, and say so, and I will redeem part of it now; and if you do not think it too heavy, then you had better see about fulfilling it.'

'So far,' said Brian, 'we do not consider it too heavy. In fact it seems so ridiculous that I suspect some treachery from you. We would not consider it heavy if you multiplied it by a hundred times...'

'Well I do not think my eric too small,' said Lugh, 'and I will guarantee as a de Danaan and before the de Danaan to ask no more and to seek no further vengeance once it is paid. Now, as I have guaranteed this before the de Danaan, I demand the same guarantee from you that you will faithfully complete this eric.'

'Are we not ourselves, and our word, sufficient guarantee,' asked Brian, suddenly angry.

'No,' said Lugh, 'you are not, for it would not be the first time that the like of you went back on the promise of a fine.'

So, unwillingly, because their word had been doubted, the sons of Tuireann agreed to be bound by solemn oath and sureties, and offered as security that they would complete their part of the fine, provided Lugh did not increase his claims, Nuada, the king of Eire, and Bodbh Dearg, the king of Connacht. And they did this before the great assembly of the Tuatha de Danaan chiefs and princes in the Hall of Moycorta in Tara.

Then Lugh said: 'Now that it is agreed and there is no going back on it, it is time to give you more detailed knowledge of the eric.'

'It is,' replied the sons of Tuireann.

'Very well,' said Lugh, 'the three apples must come from the Garden of the Hesperides in the eastern world, and none other will I have. There are no apples in all the world like them, for they are the colour of gold and have immense power and virtue. They are as big as the head of a month old child, and never grow less no matter how much is eaten from one of them. They have the taste of honey, and if a wounded man or one in deadly sickness takes a bite from one he is cured immediately. Moreover, if a warrior has one of them,

41

he can perform with it whatever feat he will, by casting it from him, and it will return to his hand. And brave though you are, Brian and Uar and Uraca, I do not think you have the ability – a matter I have no regrets about – to take these apples from those who guard them, for it has been prophesied that three young knights from the west would come to take these apples, and the king who owns them has set great guards upon them.'

He paused a moment and looked about him. The faces of everyone in the room were grim.

'The skin of the pig,' he went on, 'is that of Tuis, the king of Greece. And when this pig lived every stream through which she walked became wine thereafter for nine days, and the wound or sickness with which it would come in contact would become well. Now the druids of Greece said that it was not in the pig, but in the pig's skin, that the virtue was, so they had it flayed and preserved the skin. And that is the second part of my fine, nor do I think you will have any success in getting that. And do you know what spear I want from you?'

'We do not,' answered the Tuireann, grimly.

'It is the venomed spear of Pisear, king of Persia, and the Slaughterer it is called. And in time of peace it must be kept in a great cauldron of water to prevent it destroying the palace, and whoever carries it in wartime can do what he will with it. And that is the spear I want, and I doubt if you will get it.

'The steeds and the chariot I want are those of Dobar, king of Sicily,' said Lugh, 'the chariot that excels those anywhere in the world and the horses that, no matter how often they are killed, will come to life again if their bones are brought together in the same place. You will not get these easily, if at all.

'The seven pigs I demand,' he went on, 'are the pigs of Easal, king of the Golden Pillars which, though killed every day, will be found alive again the following day; and the hound-pup is the property of the king of Iora. Failinis is the name of the pup and so great is her power that the wild beasts of the forests fall down helpless before her. And the cooking spit I require is one from the island of Fiancara, protected by the warlike women of the island, any one of whom is able for three champions such as you. And the hill on which you must give the three shouts is the Hill of Mokeen in Lochlann; and Mokeen and his family are solemnly bound not to permit a shout to be given on the hill, and are constantly on guard against it. It was with them, moreover, that my father recieved his education and, even if I were to forgive you, you may be sure that they would not. And even if you were to succeed in all the rest of the eric, then they will make sure to avenge my father's death.

'And this, sons of Tuireann, is the eric I ask of you.'

CHAPTER FOUR

Astonishment and despair settled on the children of Tuireann when they heard the terms of the eric. But, together and silent, they stood up and, without saying a word left the great hall of Moycorta and went to their father's house and told him what had happened.

Tuireann was worried and upset, but he gave the following advice to his sons.

'Your news is dreadful,' he said, 'and I cannot see how you can escape death and destruction in carrying out this eric-fine; but, hard as it is for me to say it, it seems that your punishment is a just one for it was an evil thing to kill Cian. Now as far as the fine itself is concerned, no living man can get it without the help of either Lugh himself or of Mananaan. Therefore go to Lugh now and ask him to lend you Mananaan's horse, Aonvarr of the Flowing Mane, and he will not give it to you; what he will say is that it does not belong to him and that he would not give the loan of a loan away. Then ask him for Mananaan's boat, the Wave-Sweeper – which will be of more use to you anyway – and he will not refuse you that, for he is solemnly forbidden to refuse a second request.'

So the sons of Tuireann went to Lugh and asked him for the steed, and Lugh replied as their father had said he would:

'The horse is not my own,' said Lugh, 'and I cannot lend what I only have on loan myself.'

'In that case,' said Brian, 'lend us the Wave-Sweeper of Mananaan.'

Lugh was angry when he saw how he had been tricked, but there was nothing he could do about it.

'Very well,' he said, 'she lies at Brugh na Boinne, the harbour of the Boyne and you have my permission to take her.'

So the sons of Tuireann returned once more to their father's castle where Tuireann and their sister Eithne were waiting for them, and told them that Lugh had given them the boat.

'Much good it will do you, I'm afraid,' said Tuireann, 'except that it is better than nothing at all. Clearly Lugh wants as much of the eric as will be of use to him at the coming battle of Moytura, otherwise he would have found ways of thwarting you in your second request also. He may help you in getting those things for him. But for the things that are of no use to him, and much danger to you, he will give you no help and be all the more satisfied if ye get killed while attempting them.'

The three young warriors took their leave of their father and went to the Boyne harbour where the boat lay moored. Their sister Eithne went to bid them farewell.

When Brian saw the boat, he was horrified, for instead of the large seagoing ship he had expected, he found it was no more than a quite small currach, or open canoe.

Bitterly he kicked at it and said: 'What use is this to us, even if more than two of us would fit in it?'

But his words alarmed Eithne, who warned him that the currach was a magic one and would adapt itself to suit whatever was necessary to be carried in it; furthermore it was forbidden to grumble at it. And she went on to say:

'You had no right, my brothers, much as I love you, to do what you did, and I am afraid that nothing but evil will come of it.' Then they exchanged the following verses:

> *Eithne:*
> 'It was an evil thing to do
> For you three, fair and generous.
> The noble father of the noble Lugh
> To kill: and the evil on all of us.'

The Sons:
'Oh Eithne do not say that,
Keen our hearts, brave our deeds;
Rather death a hundredfold
Than to live cowardly weeds.'

Eithne:
'Search the lands and islands
To the limits of the Red Sea;
Your banishment from Ireland
Is a great sadness for me.'

After this the three brothers entered the canoe, which, as Eithne had said, grew as large as was necessary to accomodate them and their gear, and bidding a last farewell to their grief-stricken sister, sailed out on the open sea.

'Now,' said Uar and Uraca,' what course will we take first?'

'The apples,' said Brian, 'for they are what Lugh asked for first. And so,' he said addressing the currach, 'we command you, Wave Sweeper of Mananaan, take us without delay to the Garden of the Hesperides.'

And, as always, the currach responded directly to the voice of whoever commanded it, and it bounded forward across the bosom of the gren-crested waves, more swiftly than the winds of spring, it took the shortest sea route and did not stop until it reached harbour near the Garden of the Hesperides.

Then Brian said: 'Now, how do you think we ought to go to the Garden of the Hesperides, for it seems to me that it is bound to be well guarded and probably with the king himself at the head of the guards?'

'Since we are bound to be killed sooner or later in paying this eric,' said his brothers, 'perhaps it would be best to get it over and done with now. Therefore maybe the best way would be to go forward and attack them and if we succeed well and good, and if not we might be just as well off to die here.'

'Brave, but foolish words,' said Brian, 'and soldiers should be wise and intelligent as well as brave. Let us do this so that people can say afterwards of us that we were prudent and skillful as well as valiant, so that they will respect our cunning and not despise our stupidity. It seems to me that the most sensible thing for us to do in this case is to turn ourselves into the appearance of hawks and sweep into the garden. The guards will only be able to use their light weapons against us, and let you make sure to avoid them and be prepared for them. Then, when they have fired all they have at us, let us sweep down and carry off an apple each, and I will try to take two if I can.'

So that is what they did. Brian truck each of them with his druid's wand and transformed them into the appearance of hawks of incomparable beauty and speed, which made off towards the garden immediately. When they reached it they circled and hovered high in the sky for a moment, and then began to descend in spirals. But the guards spotted them and attacked them with great showers of missiles, which the three brothers dodged and evaded until all the guards ammunition was gone. Then, swooping suddenly down on the glittering trees, the two younger brothers carried off an apple each and Brian took one in his talons and one in his beak, and they rose again into the air without having been wounded or touched. Then they turned westward again and raced for the place where they had left the Wave Sweeper.

But the news had already reached the court of the king who had three daughters who were cunning sorceresses. They immediately transformed themselves into three griffins and pursued the hawks out to sea, and they threw great tongues of fire after them and around them from their open screeching mouths, which overtook the hawks and burnt and blinded them so that they could bear the heat no longer.

'We're finished now,' said Uar and Uraca, 'unless we can get out of this.'

'I'll see what I can do,' said Brian, and tapped his brothers and himself with the druid's wand which this time turned them into three swans and they flew below to the sea. When the griffens found that the hawks were gone they gave up the pursuit, for they were not very intelligent, and the sons of Tuireann made their way back to the Wave Sweeper.

CHAPTER FIVE

After resting awhile they decided that, since it was not too far away, that they would go to Greece to seek the skin of the pig and bring it away either by guile or by force. So they commanded the currach to take them to a harbour close to the palace of Tuis, the king of Greece.

When they reached landfall Brian asked:

'In what form do you think it best that we should go to this court?'

'In what other form would we go her,' replied Uar and Uraca, 'but in our own.'

'I disagree,' said Brian, 'It seems to me that the wisest thing to do here would be to disguise ourselves as poets and learned men from Eire, for poets and scholars are held in high honour by the noble Greeks.'

'That's all very well,' replied Uar and Uraca, 'but where are we if we're asked to show our skill? We haven't a poem between us, and still less do we know how to compose one.'

'More fools you,' said Brian, 'for not learning both when you had the opportunity.'

Nevertheless he persuaded them and, putting the knots of poets in their hair they approached the palace gates. The guards asked what they wanted.

'We are poets from Eire,' replied Brian, 'who have come with a poem for the king.'

One of the guards reported this to King Tuis, who said:

'Bring them in, for if they have come so far in search of a patron then they may have found him.'

Now the king commanded that the court should be made even more splendid than it already was to receive these foreign poets so that when they left they could tell the world that it exceeded anything they knew for grandeur. And so, when all was ready, the three sons of Tuireann in the guise of poets, were admitted to where the king sat, surrounded by his nobles, in the glittering banqueting hall. Bowing low the three warriors greeted the king, who saluted them in return and welcomed them. The king invited them to join the feast, which they did, and never had they seen a household so full of merriment, a banquet so splendid or a palace more magnificent.

Then, according to custom, the king's own poets arose to recite their poems for the king and the guests and when they were finished, Brian, speaking low, said to his brothers:

'We must make a poem for the king also.'

'We have no poems,' they replied, 'therefore how can we recite one for the king. Ask us to fight like warriors, as you have taught us, or to fall if they are stronger than we are, but to make a poem...'

So Brian, giving them a look of disgust, said: 'That is not the way to compose a poem.' Then he stood up himself and asked for attention while he sang his own poem, which was this:

> 'Your fame we sing of, Oh Tuis,
> Great as an oak among kings,
> A pigskin, reward without meanness,
> We claim in return for our songs.

> 'In the war of a neighbour, an ear,
> And the ear of a neighbour shall clash
> But he who gives without fear
> Shall lose nothing, not having been rash.

> 'A hot host and tempestuous sea
> Are weapons that one would oppose;
> A pigskin, reward given free,
> It is that that we claim from you, Tuis.'

'That,' said the king, 'is a very good poem, I daresay, but I don't understand one word of it.

'I will interpret it for you,' said Brian.

'Your fame we sing of Oh Tuis, great as an oak among trees... that means that you excel all other kings in nobleness, generosity and greatness just as the oak excels the other trees of the forest. A pigskin, reward without meanness, we claim in return for our songs... that means what it says, that you have the skin of a pig that I want to get from you as a reward for my poem, and in the war of a neighbour an ear, and the ear of a neighbour shall clash... means that, unless you give it to me willingly, you and I will be about each others ears. And that is what my poem means,' concluded Brian.

The king sat back and looked at him in wonder at what

he said. For there was Brian with his two brothers, while the king was surrounded by a host of nobles, friends and soldiers.

'I would praise your poem,' he said, 'if you had not mentioned my pigskin. And you seem to be a very foolish man, oh poet, to ask for that skin, for, if all the poets and scholars of Eire, and all the chiefs and nobles of the whirling world were to demand it of me, I would refuse them, unless they took it from my by force. Nevertheless, you will not go unrewarded, and I will give you three times that skin full of red gold in payment for your poem.'

'You are generous, oh king,' said Brian, 'and good luck and good health to you for it. I knew I would get something worthwhile if I asked for what I did boldly. But I am a suspicious man by nature and will not accept your offer, lest your servants cheat me in the measuring, unless I see them measuring the gold from the skin with my own eyes.'

The king agreed to this and so his servants took the three sons of Tuireann to the treasure house to measure the gold, and one of them brought the skin from its special place to be filled.

'Measure the two skinfuls for my brothers first,' said Brian then to the man with the pigskin, 'and give me the last measure, for it was I who made the poem.' And satisfied with what he said the man turned to do as Brian told him, but as he turned Brian grabbed the skin with his left hand and drawing his sword with his right hand, cut the man clean in two with it. He wrapped the skin about himself and turning with his brothers rushed back through the palace attacking everyone they met on their way until they reached the banqueting hall again. There the nobles, seeing how things were, surrounded and attacked them, but the three sons of Tuireann, their battle fury on them and in raging desperation, hewed them down wherever they happend to come, so that not a noble, nor a champion nor a warrior escaped being slaughtered, mutilated or injured.

At last Brian fought his way to where King Tuis was, and the king attacked him with great courage and strength. But brave though he was, and strong though he was he was no match for Brian, and he eventually fell to the eldest son of Tuireann.

As for Uar and Uraca, they killed and slaughtered all

round them until there was no more killing or destruction to be done and none were left save the women and the servants, the dead and the wounded. Then the three sons of Tuireann rested there in the palace before continuing their journey in the Wave Sweeper.

While they rested they had considered the next best step to take in accomplishing their eric, and it seemed to them wisest to go to the kingdom of Pisear, the Persian king, for the blazing spear.

So, they left the blue-washed shores of Greece and commanded the currach to take them eastward into Persia. And as they went Brian reminded his brothers that now that they had the apples from the Garden of the Hesperides and the pigskin from Tuis, it might not be so difficult to acquire the spear. Furthermore, although Uar and Uraca were not all that happy about it, they agreed that the disguise of poets had served them well and they proposed to remain in that disguise at Pisear's court.

And, just as happened when they came to the palace of Tuis, they were welcomed and admitted to the banqueting hall where King Pisear was celebrating with his nobles and chief people. They were seated with distinction and after a time the king's poets arose and began to recite their poems for the assembly. When they had finished Brian again said to his brothers, sarcastically: 'Get up now and make a poem for Pisear.'

But they said no, that they could not, but that they would fight if he asked them to.

'That would be a queer way of making a poem,' said Brian, 'but never mind, since I have my own poem for the king, I'll sing it for him now.' And he spoke this poem.

> 'Pisear has little value on spears
> For his enemies battles are broken.
> Pisear has little cause for tears
> Since it is others who receive the wounds.
>
> The yew is the finest tree in the wood
> Called king without opposition.
> May the great spear shafts make their way
> Through the wounds of those they slay.'

'That is not a bad poem,' said the king, 'but I don't understand the reference to a spear in it.'

'Because,' said Brian, 'I want to get your spear as a reward for my poem.'

'You are a foolish man,' said the king, 'to make that request, for no man has ever escaped punishment who asked me for my spear and the greatest gift I could give you, or the greatest favour these nobles here could obtain for you, is that I should spare your life.'

When Brian heard this, he remembered about the apple he had in his hand, so he threw it at Pisear and so powerful was the throw that it knocked the king's brains backwards through his head. Then Brian and his two brothers drew their swords and began to slay all around them until those that remained alive fled in terror and there was no one left in the banqueting hall except the three sons of Tuireann.

Then they searched the palace until they came to the room, in its deep recesses, where the blazing spear was kept with its head down in a great, deep cauldron of hissing and bubbling water. Then, taking up the lot, they left the palace and went back to their currach.

CHAPTER SIX

They rested for a few days after their battle, and while they were resting decided that they would next go to Sicily to take the horses and the chariot of Dobar, the king of Sicily. So, in high spirits after the success of their first three ventures, they commanded the Wave Sweeper to take them westwards to Sicily. There they landed, and Brian, carrying the great, venomed and blazing spear of Pisear in his hand, asked his brothers in what guise they should present themselves to Dobar.

'What other way but as ourselves,' they replied, 'three champions of Eire who have come to take his steeds and his chariot by force or by any other way that comes handy?'

'No,' said Brian, 'that does not seem to me the best way to go about this. But let us represent ourselves as three mercenary soldiers from Eire, willing to serve him for his

51

money. In that way we will learn how and where the horses and chariot are kept and guarded.'

So, having agreed to this, the three of them set out for the palace.

Now it so happened that the king and all his subjects were attending a great fair on the plain before the palace, and the three warriors came near the crowds drew back and made way for them so that they were able to walk straight up to the king. They bowed and paid homage to him and he asked them who they were and where they came from.

'We are soldiers from Eire,' replied Brian, 'seeking service and pay among the kings of the world.'

'And will you serve me for a while,' asked Dobar.

'We will,' said Brian, and so they made a covenant and compact with the king... the king to place them in a post of honour and they to serve him faithfully and ask their own reward. They remained in the palace for a month and a fortnight, getting what information they could and familiarising themselves with the places of the island, but they saw or heard nothing of the steeds and the chariot during that time. And after that time Brian said:

'This isn't so good, brothers. We know no more about the horses and the chariot now than we did when we came here first.'

'Then what will we do?' they asked.

'I think,' said Brian, 'the way to deal with it is this; we will arm ourselves fully for travelling and go before the king and tell him that unless he shows us the steeds and the chariot, we will leave his service.'

This they did, and when they went to the king he asked them what was wrong and why they were dressed for travelling.

'I will tell you, Dobar,' said Brian, 'soldiers of Eire, such as we are, are accustomed to be the most trusted guards and champions of the kings they serve, and their most precious possessions; and in addition they are counsellors and advisors as well. But you did not treat us like that, Dobar, for we have learned that you have a chariot and two steeds which are the best in the world, and yet we have not even seen them.'

'If that is all that bothers you,' said the king, 'it is an easy matter to adjust, and there is no need for you to leave my service. Indeed I would have shown them to you on the first day if I had known that you wanted to see them, but I shall show them to you now. For I never had in this court or in my service soldiers in whom I had greater trust.'

Then he sent for the steeds and for the chariot and yoked them to it, those steeds that were faster than the winds of March and equally swift across land or water. And Brian, who was eyeing them carefully, said:

'Now listen to me Dobar, King of Sicily. We have served you faithfully up to now, and now we wish to name our pay according to the covenant that we made with you; and it is this that we demand, those steeds and chariot, these we mean to have, and nothing else.'

Then the king in terrible anger said: 'Foolish and luckless men! You shall certainly die because of your presumption.' And the king and all his men turned towards the three sons of Tuireann to kill them.

But Brian, watching his opportunity, sprang into the chariot, hurled the charioteer to the ground, and took up the reins in his left hand. Then, raising the blazing spear of Pisear in his right hand, he decimated the hosts of Dobar so that the king and his men were killed with great slaughter by himself and Uar and Uraca, and those who were not killed, fled. Then, taking their prize with them, they returned again to the Wave Sweeper.

After resting awhile until their wounds were healed, they decided that next they would go to Asal, king of the Golden Pillars, to search for the seven pigs which were the next part of the fine that the Il-Dana had put upon them.

And so they sailed forthwith towards the land of the Golden Pillars in the Wave Sweeper, but as they came towards the shore they saw that it was lined with armed men, and every harbour was strongly fortified, for the fame and the the news of the great deeds of the sons of Tuireann had travelled before them throughout the countries of the world; of their being banished from Eire and of their seeking and carrying off the gifted jewels of the world. And it was because of this that Asal's men guarded his shores so thoroughly.

Asal himself came down to the harbour to meet them as they sailed in and when they were close enough he told them to stay their course; and then he asked them sadly if it was true that it was by them that so many kings of the world had fallen in every land in which they had been. Brian replied that it was true, whatever he might wish to inflict on them for it if he could.

'What reason have you for it,' asked Asal.

Then Brian told him that they had no choice in the matter. 'It is the fault of the Il-Dana,' he said, 'and of the unjust sentence which he has imposed on us and which we are bound to pay. If the kings to whom he had sent us had given freely the precious things we sought we would have departed in peace; but as they did not, we fought against them, unwillingly it is true, and overthrew them, for none was able to stand against us.'

'And why have you come here,' asked Asal.

'For the seven pigs you have,' replied Brian, 'for they are part of the fine.'

'And how will you get them,' asked Asal.

'If we get them in token of your kindness and friendship, then we will take them thankfully; but if not, then we will fight for them and either bring them with us by force after killing you and your people, or we will fall ourselves in the attempt.'

'If that were to be our fate, like that of Greece and Persia and Sicily,' said Asal, 'then it would be unfortunate indeed for us to give battle.'

'Indeed,' said Brian, 'it might.'

Then the king went into council with his chiefs, and, having debated the situation at length, they decided to give the pigs to the sons of Tuireann of their own free will since no king, however powerful, had as yet been able to withstand them.

When the three champions heard this they were overcome with wonder and amazement at the wisdom of the decision, for they were sick of slaughter, and gave gratitude and thanks to Asal, as much for his wisdom in granting them the pigs without battle and bloodshed, as in relief for getting one part of the fine without losing a great deal of their own blood in the process.

That night Asal entertained them in his palace where they were welcomed and feasted and provided with comfortable beds to rest in. On the following day they were escorted to the king's presence and the pigs were handed over to them. Then Brian sang a poem in praise of Asal's wisdom and generosity.

'And where,' asked Asal, 'do you propose to go next, sons of Tuireann?'

'We'll go,' said Brian, 'to Iora for the hound-pup, Failinis, which is another part of the eric that the Il-Dana has put on us.'

'Then do me a favour,' said Asal, 'take me with you to Iora, for my daughter is the king's wife and I will do what I can to persuade him to give you the pup without battle.'

The sons of Tuireann agreed to this, but King Asal, being the prudent man he had shown himself to be, didn't much care for the look of Mananaan's frail currach for such a journey in spite of it's marvellous qualities, and he insisted on going in his own ship. This was prepared and with great pomp and ceremony the great ship and the small currach sailed together out of the harbour of the land of the Golden Pillars and sailed for Iora, and their adventures on that journey, if any, are not related.

But when they reached Iora their fame and prowess had again gone before them and the entire shore was lined with fiercely armed men who shouted at them warning them to come no further, because they knew the sons of Tuireann and what they had come for.

Asal advised the three warriors to remain at anchor where they were and said that he would go ashore and try to persuade his son-in-law, the King of Iora, to be sensible. So Asal himself went peacefully ashore and was taken respectfully to the palace of the king of Iora. This king asked him what brought the sons of Tuireann to his country.

'They want the hound-pup that you have,' replied Asal.

'You showed little sense in accompanying them then,' said the king to Asal, 'for there aren't three warriors in the entire world to whom the gods have given enough strength or good luck as to take that pup, either by force or goodwill.'

This attitude upset Asal, and he pointed out that wherever the three sons had been, they had left death and destruction behind them no matter what the opposition, except in his own land and that was because he had given the seven pigs freely.

'They have overpowered and slain great kings,' he said, 'for they have arms that no warrior, however powerful, can withstand; and I urge you to take my advice and give them the hound-pup in peace.'

But his words were wasted on the king of Iora who was full of fiery words and anger, and the troubled Asal went and told the sons of Tuireann how matters stood.

Then Brian and his brothers armed themselves and declared war on the king and warriors of Iora and a terrible and bloody battle began on the shore as they landed from the currach.

For, though nothing could stand against the sons of Tuireann, the army of the Iora was great and its warriors brave. And the battle became so fierce and confused that the three brothers became separated from one another, Uar and Uraca being driven away from Brian where he wielded tremendous death and destruction on all who crossed his path with the blazing spear of Pisear. At last, through the din and the smoke of the battle, Brian spied the battlepen of the king of Iora, surrounded by his guards, and he fought his way towards it and no man in his path could stand against him so great was his battle-fury. When he reached the battle pen he burst in upon it like a thunderbolt and, although the king put up a powerful and venemous defence, Brian, though by far the more wrathful and the stronger, held back so as not to slay his enemy, but prolonged the combat to tire him. When he then had an opportunity he seized the king and bound him with his arms and carried him aloft to where Asal was. Throwing the king down at Asal's feet, Brian said:

'There is your son-in-law for you and I swear, by my weapons, it would have been easier to kill him three times over than to bring him alive to you like this.'

When the army of Iora saw their king defeated and a prisoner they threw down their arms. Peace was made between them and the sons of Tuireann, and the hound-pup was handed over to the three warriors from Eire. Then they took their leave of Iora in friendship with its king and people and Asal, to whom they bade farewell with kindness and regret.

CHAPTER SEVEN

Lugh, meanwhile, had been following the successes of the sons of Tuireann with mixed feelings. He was kept closely informed of all that happened through his own mystical powers and now he was aware that they had acquired all those parts of the eric he had put on them which would be of use to him in the forthcoming battle of Moytura, but that they had not yet got the cooking-spit or given the three shouts on the Hill of Mokeen. Accordingly he wove a spell and sent it after them which, falling on them as they sailed from Iora in the Wave Sweeper, made them forget the remaining part of the fine and filled them with an immense homesickness. Therefore, satisfied that they had fulfilled the eric, they commanded the currach to return to Eire with all possible speed.

Now it so happened that when the Wave Sweeper reached the shore of Eire at Brugh na Boinne again, Lugh was with Nuada at a great fair on the plain before the city of Tara. It was revealed to him through his extraordinary powers that the sons of Tuireann had landed on the Boyne, and he immediately left the fair and, telling no one, went to the fort of Cathair Crofinn, closing the mighty gates and doors after him. There he armed himself fully in the armour of Mananaan and the magical cloak of the daughter of Fleas and waited.

Soon afterwards the sons of Tuireann were seen approaching the fair and as they did so the great multitude flocked out to meet them gazing in wonder at the things they brought and to welcome them home. Nuada himself greeted them warmly and asked them if they had fulfilled the eric.

'We have,' they replied, 'and where is Lugh that we may give it to him?'

'He was here a little while ago,' said Nuada. But the fair was searched for Lugh without success.

Then Brian said: 'I know what has happened. He has learned that we have returned with these great weapons against which even he himself could not stand, and he has barricaded himself in one of the strongholds of Tara for fear we might turn them on him.'

Messengers were then sent to search for Lugh to tell him that the sons of Tuireann had the eric he demanded and were ready to give him the fine. But Lugh still did not trust the sons of Tuireann, and the answer he sent back was that the fine should be given to Nuada for him.

The sons of Tuireann did as Lugh demanded, and turned their marvellous spoils over to the king there on the lawn before the palace, keeping only their own arms. When Lugh had been satisfied that things had been done as he required, he came out and inspected the eric narrowly.

'Here indeed,' he said, 'is eric fine enough to pay for anyone who ever has been killed and anyone who ever will be killed to the end of time; but nevertheless and notwithstanding that it is great, and many times great, there is one kind of fine that must be paid in full to the last iota, and that is an eric-fine, for of this it is not lawful to hold back even the smallest part. And moreover, King Nuada and King Bodbh Dearg, and you people of the de Danaan, you are guarantee for my full eric fine; therefore while I see here the three apples, the skin of the pig, the blazing spear, the chariot and the steeds, the seven pigs and the hound pup – where, sons of Tuireann, is the cooking spit of Fincara; and I did not hear that you gave the three shouts on the hill of Mokeen.'

When they heard this a great weakness overcame the sons of Tuireann and they fell to the ground as if they were dead. They lay in this stupor for a while and, when they recovered they spoke no word, but left the fair and went straight to their father's castle at Howth. To him and to Eithne they told what had happened and that, having thought they were safe and rid of the eric, they now had to set off on another voyage to complete it.

Having spent the night with their father and sister, the three sons prepared to set sail in their ship next day – for they no longer had the benefit of the Wave Sweeper to take them wherever they wished to go. They sailed out of Dublin Bay, with the Hill of Howth on one hand, and Wicklow Head on the other, and made across the loud-murmuring sea in search of the Island of Fiancara. For three months they searched the ocean, landing at this country and that and on one island and another one, but could not get the least information about Fiancara. At last they met an old, old man; toothless and almost eyeless, for they were hidden in his head with folds of flesh about them like the shell of a walnut, and he told them that in his youth he had heard of this island of Fiancara, but that it lay not on the surface of the sea, but down deep in the seething waters where it was sunk because of a spell put on it in times long past.

Then Brian put on his diving suit with its helmet of clear glass and, telling his brothers to wait his return, he leaped over the side of the ship and sank from sight. It is said that he was a whole fortnight walking the bed of the salt water seeking the Island of Fiancara before he found it.

When he did so he found it to have many houses, but one great palace more noble than all the rest and to this he immediately went. When he reached it he found that its doors stood open so he entered and found inside nothing but a group of women, all very beautiful, engaged at needlework and embroidery; and among them, lying on a table, was a cooking spit.

When Brian saw it he said not a word, but walked straight to the table, siezed the spit and turned and walked towards the door. The women neither spoke nor moved, but each had her eyes fixed on him from the moment he entered admiring his manly bearing and fearlessness; but when they saw him walking off with the spit they burst out laughing, and one of them said:

'You are a brave man, Brian, to attempt what you are. But, even if your two brothers were with you, the weakest of us – and there are a hundred and fifty of us here – could by herself prevent the three of you from taking the spit. Nevertheless, you are brave and courageous to make the attempt knowing the danger and, for thy boldness and valour, and the manliness you show, we will let you take this one for we have many more besides.'

So Brian, having thanked them and made his farewells, left them and went to find his brothers. Uar and Uraca had stayed anchored in the one place while Brian was away, fearing that if they moved they might lose him for good. At last they began to be afraid that he was lost and were about to draw anchor and set their sails when they saw the glitter of his helmet rising towards them from the bosom of the waves. Brian himself followed up through the sea and they were overjoyed when they saw him clutching the cooking spit in his hand.

When Brian had told them all that had happened he rested awhile before setting out for the Hill of Mokeen, for they knew that here they would be likely to have their most difficult task. They turned the prow of their ship northwards and sailed in that direction until at last they saw the green hill rising smooth and lofty from the shore. When Mokeen saw them approaching he knew at once who they were and, wading into the sea he shouted at them:

'It was you who killed my friend and foster-brother Cian; and now you come here to shout upon this hill; well come out of your ship for you will not leave these shores alive.'

When Brian heard this he was consumed with an almighty rage and he leaped ashore and the two great warriors attacked each other ferociously; so great, indeed was their onslaught on each other that it can be compared only to the fury of two bears, or the laceration of lions or the savagery of great beasts, until at length Mokeen fell dead.

And then the three sons of Mokeen came out to fight the three sons of Tuireann. And so a fight began that surpassed all the fights that ever were or were ever told of; so great was the noise of it that the waves receded from the edge of the mountain and curled back in terror; the very mountain itself, across whose face they struggled and let flow each others blood, split and sundered and poured forth the fire of its heart, and the sky blackened with smoke and reddened with flame, so that if a man were in the east as far as the Hesperides, or in the west as far as the world's end, then he would come in awe and wonder to see such mighty blows being given and received.

Finally, after three days of great combat and shaking the mountain with their stamping feet, the three sons of Mokeen put their three spears through the bodies of the three sons of Tuireann. But neither fear nor weakness did this bring to the heroes, for they in turn put their three spears through the bodies of the sons of Mokeen, who fell dead before them on the battlefield.

But now that the combat was over and their battle-fury had passed off, the three sons of Tuireann fell to the ground themselves, lying on the blood-stained grass, and remained there for three days without moving or speaking a word as if they were dead; a heavy curtain of darkness veiling their eyes.

At last Brian revived and, seeing his brothers lying where they had fallen, said feebly:

'Brothers, how are you?'

'We are dead,' they replied, 'or as near it as makes no difference.'

'Get up,' said Brian, 'my poor brothers and make the three shouts on the hill before death claims us.'

But they were unable to do it. So Brian, gathering together all his remaining strength, lifted one of them in each arm even while the life's blood flowed in rivers from him, and they raised three feeble shouts on the Hill of Mokeen.

Then Brian, still supporting the other two, staggered to the ship and they fell on board and turned her prow towards Eire. For days the ship moved across the ocean without guidance save its own, but drifted all the time towards Eire. And, while they were still far off, Brian lifted his head and gazed across the sea to the west and suddenly cried:

'I see Ben Eadair, the Hill of Howth, and the fort of Tuireann, rising from the waters.'

And Uar, from where he lay for he had not the strength to lift himself, said: 'Oh Brian, if only we could see them; and on your honour and from your love for us, raise our heads on your breast that we can and after that it makes no difference if we live or die.'

Then they sang this lament:

'Lift our heads, Brian, on your breast,
Son of Tuireann, generous and red-armed;
Oh torch of valour without deceit,
That we may see Eire again
Raise to your breast and your shoulder
These heads, oh soldier hero,
That we may see before us from the water
Usna, and Tailteann and Tara
Dublin and the smooth Boyne with you;
If we should see Howth before us
With Castle Tuireann to the north
We would welcome death from that onward,
Even if it were a suffering death.'

Brian:
'It is a tragedy, sons of brave Tuireann;
Birds could fly through my two sides
Yet it is not my sides that make me suffer,
But that you both have fallen.'

'We would prefer death to take us
Brian, son of Tuireann,
Than to see the wounds on your body
Without doctors to cure you.
And since there are none here to cure us —
Miach, Omiach or Diancecht —
It is tragic, Brian, who suspected no deceit,
To have parted with the healing pigskin.'

So Brian lifted them in his arms so that they could see Howth hill as the ship drifted into the harbour under its craggy slopes. Slowly and in great pain they made their way to Castle Tuireann and Brian called out as soon as he was near enough.

'Father, take the spit and go to Lugh as quickly as possible and tell him that we have given the three shouts on Mokeen's hill. Tell him that we have now paid the full eric price and bring back from him the apples of the Garden of the Hesperides, otherwise we will surely die.'

But Tuireann answered sadly:

'If all the jewels of the world, south and north,
Were given to Lugh to ease his wrath
It would not be enough to save
You from the sepulchre and the grave.'

'We are one in flesh and blood
To the son of Cian, son of just Cainte;
He will not deal us blood for blood
Even though we killed his father.
Oh father do not delay in going,
Or be long in returning,
For if you are you will not find us
Alive when you get back.'

So Tuireann mounted his chariot and drove at a gallop to

Tara so that his horses were covered in lather that flew about him like foam as he went, and the sods of the earth rose high behind him like a flock of birds. He found Lugh and gave him the cooking spit and said:

'My sons have now paid the full fine, having given the three shouts on Mokeen's hill. But they are mortally wounded and will die unless you give me the magic pigskin to cure them with.'

But Lugh refused him coldly and turned away.

So Tuireann returned sadly to his three sons and told them what had happened. Then Brian, for all his weakness, said:

'Take me with you to Tara, and I will see him, and maybe then he will relent and save us.'

So Tuireann laid him in his chariot and returned to Tara where they found Lugh. But when Brian begged for the skin to save himself and his brothers, Lugh said:

'I will not give it. If you offered me the breadth of the entire world of red gold, I would not give it, unless I thought your death would follow. You killed my father cruelly and with nothing less than your own death will I be satisfied.'

So, having done what he could to persuade the Il-Dana to relent, Brian returned to his dying brothers and lay down between them and as he did so the three of them gave a united sigh, and their lives departed from them at the same instant.

Then Tuireann and his daughter Eithne stood hand in hand over the dead heroes, and sang a lament for their dead.

Having done so, Tuireann and Eithne were so grief-stricken, that they fell beside the bodies of the three young men and died with them, so that they were all interred in the one grave.

That, then, is the tragedy of the Sons of Tuireann.

The Wooing of Etain

Many thousands of years ago, after the Milesians had come to Ireland and the Tuatha de Danaan had retired to their mystic forts from their domination, Etain of the Horses was the wife of Midhir the mystic lord of Bri Leith. Now Midhir also had another wife, which was the custom in those days, called Fuamnach, who was consumed with jealousy of the beautiful Etain and who was constantly belittling her and finding fault with her until the jealousy grew to such a canker that Fuamnach could not rest night or day until she found some means to drive Etain out of her husband's house. So she went to the unprincipled druid, Breisle Etarlamh, and between her hate and his sorcery they changed Etain into the shape of a dragon-fly that finds its pleasure among the flowers of the countryside. And when she had been changed Fuamnach raised a great wind that swept her up and out of Midhir's palace and carried her, for seven years above the world, until she came to the palace of Aengus Og, son of the Dagda Mor.

Now it so happened that, although he had been fostered by Midhir, Aengus Og was ill-disposed towards him. So, although he recognised Etain even in her transformed shape, he did not inform her husband when she was borne to him on the enchanted wind. Instead he made a crystal bower for her and filled it with flowers and fruits, with windows through which she might come and go, and he laid a purple veil in it for her and wherever he went, Aengus Og, took the bower with him.

And there, each night, she slept beside him by a means that he devised, so that she became well nourished and fairer than before; for the bower was filled with wonderfully scented shrubs, and it was upon these that she thrived, upon the scent and the blossom of the finest of precious flowers.

But Fuamnach's jealousy was still unabated and, through her witchcraft, she learned of the love that Aengus Og had for Etain. So she went to Midhir and, with great cunning, said to him:

'Why don't you ask Aengus Og to visit you, so that I may make peace between you again, and you may both then go and seek for Etain?' She knew well, of course, that Aengus Og could not bring Etain with him on this visit. So Midhir invited Aengus Og, who could not refuse such an invitiation, and he came, leaving Etain behind him. And while he was with Midhir, Fuamnach, still boiling with hatred for her enemy, searched until she found the place where Aengus Og had left Etain. And when she had found her she raised another wind like the previous one that carried Etain out of the bower and across the face of Ireland for seven years without touching the earth, in sorrow and in danger. Finally that great wind carried her above the fort of Etar the Warrior, where the men of Ulster sat at a banquet. And it so happened that Etain fell through the roof into a golden cup from which Etar's wife was drinking. And, unknown to the woman, she swallowed Etain together with the milk that was in the cup. And it so happened that as a result of this she fertilised her womb and in the course of time gave birth to an earthly child, a girl, who was given the name of Etain, daughter of Etar. And it was one thousand years in time since Etain of the Horses, who married Midhir, was born, until she was born again as the daughter of Etar.

Etain was brought up at Etar's house, and she had fifty handmaidens who were chiefs daughters constantly with her, clothed and maintained by Etar so that they would be companions for his daughter. And one day when they had gone to bathe in the river where it joins the sea, they saw a horseman riding across the plain towards them. He rode right to the water's edge and stopped to look at them bathing. The horse he rode was a great brown stallion that pranced and curvetted about the beach shaking its curly, creamy mane and tail. The horseman wore a long, flowing green cloak and a gold embroidered shirt across which the cloak was fastened with a great, golden torque that reached from shoulder to shoulder. On his back he carried a round, silver shield with a golden rim and a golden boss and in his free hand he carried a five pointed spear with bands of gold along the shaft from haft to head. His long, fair hair was swept back from his face and held in place by a circlet of gold and his eyes were calm and grey.

He sat on his dancing steed for a while gazing at the maidens, who were all filled with love for him, and then he said:

'Etain, the most beautiful of women, you are found who have been lost for many ages; wife of a king, you were swallowed by the wife of another; a heavy draught. For you a king shall wage great wars, bring destruction to the spirit world of the Sidhe and raise thousands in battle-rage; but for all your adventures and trails, Etain, you shall come to live with our folk evermore.'

And having said this, much to the wonder of the young women and their greater wonder, he went away from that place and they did not know either where he had come from or where he departed to.

Now, when Aengus Og returned to where he had left Etain and found her gone, he realised what had happened, and told Midhir;

'Fuamnach has deceived us,' said Midhir, 'and if she finds Etain she will do evil to her.'

'Indeed,' said Aengus Og, 'she may have already done so, but I will see to it that she does not escape my vengeance.'

So Aengus Og pursued her across the broad face of Ireland until he eventually found her in the retreat of the druid Breisle Etarlamh, and he took his sword and, with the one blow, struck off the heads of both of them.

When the reborn Etain was a young woman Eoai Airemon was the supreme sovereign in Ireland, for the five provinces of Ireland were obedient to him and the king of each province paid him tribute. And about a year after he became the high king he announced throughout the length and breadth of Ireland that a great festival would be held again at Tara as had been customary in the past, and he issued a royal request, which was the same as a command, that the men of Ireland should attend it bringing with them their due tributes and costoms. But the answer from the men of Ireland to this summons was:

'We will not attend the festival of Tara during such time, whether it be long or short, that the king of Ireland remains without a wife who is worthy of him.'

For there was no noble of distinction in Ireland who was without a wife; nor, they said, could any king be without a queen; nor did any man go to the festival of Tara without his wife, or any wife go without her husband.

And so, when he received this answer, Eoai, sent forth his horsemen and his scribes, his officers who commanded the roads of Ireland and the couriers and stewards of the borders of his provinces to search the country for a wife who, in her form and her grace and her countenance and her birth would be fitting for their king. And in addition there was another condition and it was that she should not have been the wife of any other man before him.

And the horsemen, and the scribes and the officers and couriers and stewards searched the country until, at last, they found a woman worthy to be the wife of Eoai, and she was Etain, daughter of Etar the Warrior who was king of Echradh. When they told Eoai about her, he went to see her for himself and bring her back with him.

But as he came near to the castle of Etar, he saw a young maiden sitting beside a stream combing her hair. The comb itself was of silver chased with gold and beside her was a silver basin also chased and embossed with golden birds, flying and sitting, and seemingly carrying in their beaks the bright beads of carbuncle with which the rim was set. She wore a beautiful purple mantle above another, a white one, ornamented with silver fringes, both clasped at her throat with a golden brooch. A green and red and golden tunic of silk with a long hood she wore as well, clasped above her breasts with clasps of gold and silver, so that men saw the bright gold and the green silk flash against the sun. On her head were two heavy tresses of flashing hair and even as Eoai saw her she was undoing it so that she could wash it, raising her arms in a graceful gesture as she did so, and bending her head sideways.

Her arms were as white as the snow of a single night, and her cheeks like the glow of a foxglove; her teeth were even and small, and gleamed like pearls between her lips, delicate and crimson. Her eyes were like the hyacinth and her shoulders high and soft and white. Tender and smooth were her wrists and her fingers long and of great whiteness with beautiful, pink nails crowning them. White as the foam of the wave her long, slender, silken-soft flanks, and her thighs smooth and white; her knees were round and her ankles straight with slim feet to set them off, and her breasts tip-tilted and firm were glorious to behold. Her eyebrows were blue-black and gently curved, and never was seen a more beautiful maiden or one more worthy of love by the eyes of man.

When Eoai saw her he was struck with a tremendous desire and love for her and he rode up to her crying:

'Who are you, young woman, and where are you from?'

'That is easy to answer,' she replied, 'I am Etain, the daughter of the king of Echradh.'

When Eoai heard this he was overjoyed and immediately told her who he was and why he had come.

'I know,' said Etain, 'and for twenty years I have waited for you, ever since I was born; and, although many men have wooed me and wished to marry me, not one of them has taken me because I have waited for you since I was a little child.'

And after that Eoai went to Etar the Warrior and paid him a great bridal price for Etain whom he brought with him back to Tara where she was welcomed like a queen.

Now Eoai had two brothers, one of whom was called Aillil and, together with all the other nobles of Ireland, he came to the Festival of Tara to meet the King's new wife. But as soon as he saw her he could not take his eyes off her for the immense love that suddenly descended on him for her. But, because she was his brother's wife, he kept his secret to himself. But, in spite of that it raged and tore and tormented him so that he became sick and weak and had to remain in Tara in one of his brother's palaces where he was looked after as well as possible, but without effect for none knew what was wrong with him. And he lay like that for a year without any indication that he was improving.

One day Eoai, who was worried about Aillil, came to see him and, putting his hand on his forehead, and said:

'How do you feel to-day?'

But Aillil only sighed.

Then Eoai said:

'Surely you must be improving by now.'

But Aillil replied: 'On my oath, as each day passes into night, it's worse I get.'

Then Eoai brought a skilled druid and physician called Fachtna to see Aillil and when he examined him, Aillil heaved another great sigh.

Then Fachtna said: 'One of two great sicknesses that kill a man and for which there is no cure is here; either the sickness of love or the sickness of envy.'

But Ailill refused to confess the reason for his illness to the physician for he was ashamed, and he was left there to die as no hope was held out for him. And he was left because Eoai had to make the royal progress throughout Ireland at that time, even though he was reluctant to leave his brother in that condition. So he said to Etain:

'While I am away take whatever care needs to be taken of Aillil. If he dies then see that he is properly mourned, that his grave mound is built and a monument put up with his name and record engraved on it.'

And Etain said that she would do this. And when Eoai was gone, Etain went every day to the room where Aillil lay and talked kindly to him and this eased his sickness as all who looked after him saw, and as long as she came to visit him he did not get worse.

Etain, of course, noticed this too and she determined to find out what it was that was wrong with him, so one day, when they were alone together, she asked him what was the cause of his sickness.

'My sickness,' he said, 'comes from my love for you.'

'And why,' she asked, 'didn't you say so before when you could have been cured long ago?'

'I could be cured even now,' he said, 'if only you would be kind to me.'

'Indeed,' she said, 'and I will be kindness itself.'

And so every day she came to visit him, bathing his head, bringing him food, and talking with him until at the end of three weeks Aillil was much better.

Then he said to her:

'You have proven your kindness to me, Etain, and I am whole again in body; but the completion of my cure at your hands is still missing; when may I have that?'

And she was greatly upset by this and by the illness that he had been through and afraid that it might strike him again, so she said:

'All that you ask you shall be given; but not in the palace of the king. Meet me at dawn to-morrow in the little wood on that hill and there your sickness will be completely cured.'

Aillil lay awake all that night in a fever of anticipation and love, but as dawn approached and the hour when he should have met Etain he fell into a deep, trancelike sleep from which he didn't waken for over three hours.

Meanwhile Etain had gone to the hill to keep the rendezvous and when she was there she saw a man approaching who looked, and spoke, and answered as if he were Aillil and so she remained with him. But when she returned to the palace and discovered Aillil in the depths of misery, she asked him what was wrong, and he told her how he had been asleep at the time of their appointment.

She said nothing to him about what had happened, though it was a great shock to her, but said:

'To-morrow is another day.'

And that night Aillil made a great fire and sat beside it so that he would not sleep, but again, as on the previous day, he fell into a trancelike sleep just before dawn from which he did not wake for several hours.

And Etain kept her rendezvous the second time, and again came the man who had the appearance and the speech of Aillil. But when she returned to the palace she found him again sorrowful because he had failed her. And three times Etain came, and three times Aillil failed to arrive, but that same man was there on each occasion. And on the third day she said to him:

'It was not to meet you that I came here, then why have you come? And as for Aillil, who was to meet me, it was not for sin or evil desire that I came to meet him, but it was just that the wife of the king of Ireland should rescue him from the sickness which oppressed him for so long.'

Then the stranger looked at her and said:

'It was more suitable for you to meet me, for when you were Etain of the Horses, it was I, Midhir, who was your husband.'

'And what caused us to be parted?' asked Etain.

'The witchcraft of Fuamnach and Breisle Etarlamh,' said Midhir, and then he made a great poem of surpassing loveliness, which described the country of the Sidhe in which there is no secret and no sorrow, where all is beauty and there is no sin and where love is everywhere, and he asked her to come back with him to it. But she refused.

'I will not give up the kingdom of Ireland for you,' she said, 'a man who knows not his clan nor his kindred.'

Then Midhir told her that it was he who, long before, had put the sickness of love on Aillil, so that his blood ceased to run and his flesh fell away from him; and that it was he also who closed his eyes with sleep so that no dishonour would fall on Etain.

'But will you come with me,' he asked, 'if Eoai should consent?'

'If such a thing happened,' said Etain in disdain, 'I would go.'

When she left Midhir she returned immediately to the room where Aillil had been, and met him outside in the lawn.

'Oh Etain,' he said, 'even though I was unable to meet you, our rendezvous has worked a wonder, for I am cured of my sickness and, moreover, your honour has not been stained.'

'It is glorious to have happend like that,' said Etain, but she said nothing of her meeting with Midhir.

In due course Eoai returned from his royal progress and was delighted to find that Aillil was fit and well again, and he particularly thanked Etain for her share in the cure, since it was well known how Aillil had improved under her care and attention.

Then one day some time later, Eoai, who had gone out very early in the morning to watch the dawn come up over the plain of Bregia, which was a most wonderful thing to see – and still is if you should chance to see it from the royal hill of Tara – beautiful with the bloom of the yellow furze, and the multicoloured hues of the different blossoms glowing in the first light. Now while he was there he saw a strange warrior close beside him on the high ground. He was a tall, straight young man, wearing a purple tunic; his long, golden hair reached to his shoulders and his eyes were lustrous and grey. In his hand he held a five pointed spear and in the other a silver shield with a golden boss. Eoai said nothing, for he knew that this young warrior had not been in Tara the night before, and the gates to the outer wall had not yet been opened except his own private entrance.

Then the warrior came and placed himself under Eoai's protection.

'Welcome,' said Eoai, 'to the hero whose name I do not yet know.'

'Your welcome is no more than I would expect from a king,' said the warrior.

'Yet I still do not know you,' said Eoai.

'But I know you well,' replied the warrior.

'What is your name?' asked Eoai.

'My name,' said the warrior,' is not famous. I am Midhir of the Sidhe.'

'And what do you want?' asked Eoai.

'I came,' said Midhir, 'to play a game of chess with yourself.'

'Well indeed,' said Eoai, 'I'm a fair hand at the chess.'

'Well, then,' said Midhir, 'let's see how good you are.'

'No,' said the king, 'because the queen is still asleep and my chessboard is in her room.'

'I have here,' said Midhir, 'a chessboard which is not inferior to your own.'

And that was true, for the chessboard was of silver and the men to play it two kinds of gold, red and white; and the board itself was divided into squares by costly jewels. So Midhir then set out the board and asked Eoai to play.

'I will not,' said Eoai, 'unless we play for a stake.'

'Well, what stake do you suggest?' asked Midhir.

'It's indifferent to me,' said Eoai.

'Very well then,' said Midhir, 'if I lose I will give you fifty dark grey horses, with chestnut dappled heads; high eared and broad chested; wide nostrilled and slender hooved, strong, eager and spirited, but well broken for all that.'

They played several games, but since Midhir did not put forth his great skill, all the victories went to Eoai. But instead of the horses which Midhir had offered, Eoai demanded that Midhir and his people should perform services which would benefit his realm; that they should clear away the rocks and stones from the plains of Meath, remove the bogs from his fortress of Teave, cut down the forest of Bregia and finally make a road across the bog of Lamhrach. And all these things Midhir agreed to do under the supervision of one of Eoai's stewards. And, that evening, the steward came and saw that Midhir and all his people were at this work with oxen, and that it was nearly completed.

And it is a fact that it is from this thing that Eoai is most remembered, for when the steward went to see Midhir and his people at work he noticed that the oxen were harnessed about the shoulders.

Now it was the custom in Ireland at that time for the men of the country to harness their oxen with a strap over their foreheads so that the pull might be against their heads. But when it was seen that the Sidhe people placed the yoke upon the shoulders of the oxen so that the pull might be there, Eoai commanded that his oxen should be yoked in the same way, and that is how he got his full name, Eoai Airemnech, or Eoai the Ploughman.

The people of the Sidhe laboured all that day at the tasks Eoai had demanded of them and, at nightfall, they were completed and the steward went in great wonder to Eoai and told him so and, that not alone was the work completed, but that it was incomparable. And as he was speaking Midhir came before them and his face was angry and as black and scowling as a thunder-cloud.

Eoai greeted him.

'Cruel and senseless is what you asked Eoai,' said Midhir, 'and you have caused much hardship and suffering to my people to make them work like this. All that you asked I have done, but you have made me angry with your requests.'

'Well,' said Eoai, 'I have no anger against you.'

'Very well then,' said Midhir, 'let us play another game of chess.'

'What stakes will we play for,' said Eoai.

'Let the winner decide,' said Midhir.

'Very well,' said Eoai, confident that he would win again.

But this time Midhir used his full skill and defeated Eoai decisively.

'My stake is forfeit to you,' said Eoai.

'And would have been long ago if I wished it,' said Midhir

'What is it that you want?' asked Eoai.

'To hold Etain in my arms and get a kiss from her,' said Midhir.

Eoai was outraged; but he kept silent for a while, while he was thinking.

'Very well,' he said then, 'a month from to-day come to Tara and you will get what you ask.'

Now Midhir had allowed Eoai to win at first so that Eoai might be in his debt, and that was why he had paid the great stakes that Eoai had demanded from him, and it was because of this that he had been able to insist that this game be played in ignorance of the stakes.

During the month that elapsed before Midhir was to claim his reward, Eoai called the armies and the heroes of Ireland together at Tara and placed them, ring upon ring, in defence around the entire city. And within the city itself he kept the most famous warriors of all so that the city was guarded within and without. And the king and queen were in the innermost stronghold of all which was locked and barred, for Eoai feared that a great army would come against him.

And, feeling safe and secure within this stronghold, on the appointed night he gave a great banquet to all the principal chiefs and kings who were there. Etain was pouring wine, as was her custom, when suddenly Midhir stood alone among them. Always fair and handsome, he seemed fairer and handsomer than ever that night standing in the banqueting hall surrounded by his enemies. So noble were his looks and bearing that, instead of rushing upon him, the assembled chiefs and nobles fell silent in amazement. The king, who was the first to recover, welcomed Midhir with a mixture of irony and respect.

'Your welcome is what I expected from a king,' said Midhir, 'now let you give me what you promised. It is a debt you owe me, and I, for my part, paid what I owed you.'

'I have not yet considered the matter,' said Eoai.

'You promised Etain herself to me,' said Midhir, 'and that is what I came for.' And Etain hearing these words blushed for shame.

'There is no need to blush,' said Midhir gently, 'for your marriage vows have in no way been disgraced. You resisted me when I asked you to come, and I have not come for you until Eoai permitted it. It is not any fault of yours that I am here.'

'I myself told you,' said Etain, 'that I would not give you anything unless Eoai allowed it.'

'But I will not allow you to go,' said Eoai, 'nevertheless he may put his arms around you on the floor of this house and kiss you as you are. But he will not leave here alive after...'

'Very well,' said Midhir.

Then, taking his weapons in his left hand and Etain beneath his right shoulder, he carried her off through the skylight of the palace, straight upwards.

And the hosts rose up about the king, for they felt they had been disgraced, seized their arms, and rushed outside to where the banquet hall was surrounded by the warriors. But all they saw above were two white swans circling Tara in the night, which then turned and flew off towards the Sidhe fort of Femun.

And Eoai, with an army of the men of Ireland, went to the fort of Femun and attacked it and dug it from the ground and destroyed it so that he might get Etain back again. And Midhir and his army opposed him and the men of Ireland in a long and bitter war; again and again the trenches and the battle-works that Eoai threw up around the fort were destroyed by sorties of the Sidhe, and again and again they were rebuilt. For nine long and bitter years the war continued, before Eoai's armies made their way into the fort. And when at last the inner defences fell, Midhir sent sixty women forth, all in the shape of Etain, so that none could tell which was the queen. And Eoai himself was deceived and chose, instead of Etain, her daughter Esa. And so Etain returned to Midhir in his Sidhe palace.

But some say that Eoai discovered that he had been deceived and returned again to the siege of Femun, and this time Etain made herself known to Eoai so there could be no mistake, and he carried her back to Tara where she lived from that out with the king.

The Combat at the Ford

That night Maeve summoned a council of war in her great battle tent that dominated the camp. Inside, the rich silks and skins of animals; the armour hanging from the tent-poles and the faces of the chieftains glittered in the glow from a dancing fire; but no face was as heavy and brooding as that of the warrior queen Maeve herself, for she was thinking how all her plans and her vast army was held up by this one man, Cuchullain who had killed day and night her hosts, and then her chief warriors one by one at the ford until he had slain Calatin and his twenty-seven sons, and his grandson, Gleas, and Freach the brave son of Fidech, all of whom he had killed the previous day.

And they sat and stood about her leaning on their spears to hear what she would advise or do.

But she asked them who they should send against Cuchullain on the following day, and, with one voice, they spoke the name they had been waiting to speak for weeks:

'Ferdia!'

Even though they knew that he was bound by compact not to give combat to his friend and comrade in arms, Cuchullain.

But they knew, even if it had not been proved to them over the last weeks, that there was only one champion who could meet Cuchullain with any chance of success, and that was Ferdia, the son of Damon, the son of Daire, the great and valiant warrior of the men of Domnann of Iris Domnann; the irresistable force, the battle-rock of destruction, and the foster-brother of Cuchullain. They had learned the art of fighting from the same teachers, Aoife and Uathach and Scathach the Scythian warrior queen, and were well matched in skill, in bravery, in valour and in the wielding of their arms. It was well known that to attempt a fight or combat with Ferdia wherever he might be, was like a man trying to knock the oaks of the forest with his fists, or stretching his hand forth into a serpent's lair or walking knowingly into the den of a lion, no matter what hero or champion of the world he might be, except for Cuchullain. And neither of them overmatched the other, except that Cuchullain alone could perform the feat of the Gae-Bolg which Scathach had taught to him in secret. But, to compensate for this, Ferdia was known to have a conganess, or secretly manufactured armour of the toughest horn from the eastern world, which neither arms nor a multitude of edges could pierce, and it was thought that this would protect him and bring him victory eventually in his battle with Cuchullain.

Now all the time that the champions of Connacht had been going each day to try and defeat Cuchullain at the ford, Ferdia had remained somewhat aloof from the rest of the camp. He realised that the other warriors knew that he was the only one in the camp who really stood any chance against the Hound of Ulster, and he also knew that they would begrudge him his refusal to fight Cuchullian and his foster-brother as the deaths of their own friends mounted.

For, although he would have helped them in a general war against the men of Ulster, he did not intend to fight in single combat against his friend and fellow pupil, with whom he had spent his youth, and with whom he had faced many dangers side by side against foreign enemies, Germans and Greeks alike.

And every day he sent his servants to watch the combats at the Ford and to tell him how Cuchullain was doing and to bring him word immediately if anything should happen to him, fighting alone against all the mighty men of Maeve. But every evening when his servants returned and told him of Cuchullain's successes, Ferdia was glad and proud because of what the Hound was doing.

And then, after weeks of single combat of this kind, in which Cuchullain systematically slayed or disabled her champion warriors, Maeve summoned the council of war at which it was decided to send Ferdia.

So, messengers were sent to Ferdia to bring him to Maeve's tent, for she said that she would see him herself to persuade him. But Ferdia denied, declined and refused these messengers, and refused to go with them, for he knew very well what Maeve wanted of him. When Maeve heard this she sent more messengers, but this time the satirists and revilers of Connacht so that they might make three satires against him

77

and three crushing reproaches, to mock at him and revile him and disgrace him, that they might raise three blisters on his face – blame, blemish and disgrace – that he might not find a place to lay his head in the world, if he did not come to Maeve. And that he would be shamed before the hosts of Connacht so that if he did not die of it immediately, he would die of the ignominy within a handful of days.

When Ferdia heard this, that it was proposed to disgrace him before the world, he went with them for the sake of his honour, saying:

'It is better to fall before the shafts of valour, bravery and skill than to fall by the shafts of satire, abuse and reproach.'

So he went with them to the queen's tent, and when he reached it and strode in through the glowing entrance, all who were within, including the king and the queen, great lords and nobles, rose up to receive him and he was conducted with great honour to where Maeve stood beside the king, Aillil, at the head of a banqueting table, beside a richly carved chair. Beside her was a great pile of skins and cushions and when she had greeted Ferdia she placed him sitting at her right hand and spoke kindly to him. But Ferdia resolved to offer every battle service, but not to battle with his own dear friend, and waited to see how the queen might approach the subject.

She entertained him with great dignity and honour, and a great feast was prepared. Choice, well-flavoured liquor – wine from Europe and sweet and dry mead from the cunning distillers of Ireland – were pressed on him by the lovely Finndabar, Maeve's beautiful daughter, who sat beside Ferdia and handed him every goblet that he drank, and gave him three kisses on his mouth with every cup that he took; so that he was not long in falling into an intoxication from the drink and from desire for Finndabar. It was Finndabar who gave him to taste the sweet smelling-apples of her bosom and murmured to him all the time that her darling and her chosen sweetheart of the world's men was Ferdia. And he was so dazzled with her beauty and the rewards she promised him, with the garments of a princess flowing around her, that he was ready to promise anything in life she wished.

And when Maeve saw how intoxicated he was with love for Finndabar, she began to make him great promises in return for what she wanted him to do.

'Do you know, Ferdia,' she said to him, 'why you were summoned here?'

And Ferdia, trying to collect his wits again for he realised that now he would surely need them, looked around the tent and said:

'There are many good chiefs and nobles here... and where else would I be found, but with them?'

Then Maeve said:

'That is not the only reason I asked you here, Ferdia. But I have a multitude of gifts to offer you if you will take them.'

And she listed the gifts:

'A chariot worth fifty bondmaids with steeds fit for a king, a retinue of twelve fully armed men at arms to accompany you as princes and great chiefs are accompanied; great tracts of land on the broad, fertile plains of Connacht, and a free life at my castle of Cruachan where you will be forever a guest if you so wish; the freedom for you and your descendants from tax or rent, and the right to be exempt from military expeditions for your son and grandson till the end of time; furthermore I will give you Finndabar, my daughter and Ailllil's to be your own wife, and my own most intimate friendship, if you wish it...'

'That is more than any man could want,' cried the assembled lords and nobles.

'And what do you want of me in return?' asked Ferdia.

'That you will meet Cuchullain at the ford of danger to-morrow,' said Maeve quickly and holding his eye with her own as she spoke.

Ferdia looked back at her for a moment; his head was heavy and his senses reeling and even as he tried to hold his gaze on Maeve it slipped to Finndabar beside him, who was stroking his hand with her own. But he said:

'They are great gifts; vast gifts that any man would crave for. But, as for me, you may take them back again for I will not slay my brother-in-arms, Cuchullain.'

Then Maeve concealed her anger, and smiled at Ferdia again and said.:

'Then I will do more.'

And from her queenly robe she took the brooch, more precious to her than any gift, for all the kings and queens of Connacht backwards through the cone of time had worn that brooch from the beginning, the sign and symbol of their sovereignty; and with her own royal hands she pinned the glittering jewel on Ferdia's cloak. There was as gasp of amazement from all the chiefs and nobles there assembled, and even Aillil's pale face became still paler.

'Now,' said Maeve, 'Ferdia; golden warrior of the men of Domnann, I have bestowed on you the princely dignity so that you will rank beside the king; go now and fight Cuchullain.'

But, flushed yet determined, Ferdia said:

'I cannot fight my brother-in-arms Cuchullain.'

And Maeve's rage was terrible when she heard this, but she concealed it behind her smiling face, though her whole body beneath her emerald gown quivered with the rage it contained.

'And do you not know, Ferdia,' she asked, 'that throughout the camp to-night by every fire you are the subject of joking and mockery; that you who were trained by Scathach as Cuchullain was, are afraid to meet him?'

Ferdia flushed and then grew pale when he heard this, for it was even harder to endure this taunting than it was to endure the promises she held out and the offer of the bed of Finndabar. He remained silent for a while, and then said:

'I may not fight my brother-in-arms, Cuchullain. Rather than do what you ask and turn my hand upon my friend in bitter combat, I would pick out six of your greatest champions, the best and bravest of all your host, and fight with them; all together or one at a time it would make no difference to me.'

Then Maeve's rage completely overcame her, and she looked at Ferdia for a long time; a cold, calculating, malevolent look; seeking best how to bend him to her will.

Then she said in a voice that could be heard through all the tent:

'It was true what Cuchullain said, then.'

'What was it he said, Maeve,' asked Ferdia.

'He said,' she replied, 'that he would not have thought it too great if you had been the first to fall to him at the ford. But now, he says, it would be little honour to kill you after the true heroes he has killed during the last weeks.'

When Ferdia heard this he became angry; yet if it had not been for the drink he had taken, pressed on him by Finndabar, he would not have believed it. Then he stood up with his great legs spread apart to steady him and his eyes blazing in his head, and he shouted:

'It was not right that even Cuchullain should speak of me like that. Never yet has he known cowardice or weariness in me by day or night... nor have I ever spoken badly of him. And if it is true that he said this, then I swear that I will be the first to be ready for battle at the ford to-morrow, much as I dislike doing it.'

Then he swore to do it and, with Finndabar smiling sweetly in his face and the queen on his other side standing close to him and all around the chiefs and warriors of Connacht, he made the compact; and Maeve in her turn named her six great champions that Ferdia had offered to fight instead of Cuchullain as sureties that all her promises to him would be fulfilled if he killed Cuchullain.

Now Fergus Mac Ri had been standing beside the king and when he heard this he was very worried, for Cuchullain was his foster-son and he became afraid for him if he met Ferdia. For Fergus well knew the great warrior that Ferdia was and the might of his arms and that of all the chiefs of Maeve he was by far the bravest and the best. Furthermore Fergus knew that, with the sole exception of the feat of the Gae-Bolga, everything that Scathach had taught Cuchullain, she had also taught to Ferdia who was older than Cuchullain, well-built and powerful, and riper in experience of war. So, when he heard what was happening, Fergus left Maeve's tent and caused men to harness his horses and yoke his chariot even though the night was late and the stars wheeled high in the cold heavens and, springing in, he grabbed up the reins and set off at a gallop to where Cuchullain's little camp was on the other side of the river.

Cuchullain welcomed him warmly, late as it was.

'I am rejoiced at your coming, Fergus,' he said, 'seldom enough we get the opportunity to meet on this expedition.'

'And I accept your welcome gladly, Cuchullain, foster-son and pupil,' said Fergus formally, but hurriedly in his anxiety, 'and I have come to tell you who it is that you will have to face at the ford to-morrow.'

'Who is it?'

'Your own friend, companion and fellow-pupil; your equal

in skill and bravery, the great champion of the west, in his impenetrable armour, Ferdia, son of Damon, will meet you to-morrow. And you must beware, for he is not like any of the other champions who have come to battle with you.'

'As my soul lives,' cried Cuchullian, 'I wish that he was not coming here to fight, out of my love and affection for him. And almost would I prefer to fall by his hand than that he should fall by mine.'

'I know that,' said Fergus, 'I know you dislike the thought of it; but he is coming, and of all the warriors who have come to the ford up to now, he is by far the most formidable and best prepared. Therefore rest well to-night and be prepared.'

'You have mistaken me,' said Cuchullain, 'it is not from any fear of him but from the greatness of my love for him that I think this challenge strange and unwelcome. That is the only reason I regret his coming.'

'Nevertheless, you should not think it any disgrace to fear Ferdia,' said Fergus, 'for he is the equal of ten men in combat and you should be on your guard and prepared. For he is the fury of the lion, the bursting of wrath and the blow of doom and the wave that drowns foes.'

'It's strange that you of all people, Fergus, should warn me to be careful of any man in Ireland,' cried Cuchullain. 'It's well that it was yourself and not another who said those words. From the first Monday of winter until the beginning of spring I have stood here alone,' said Cuchullain, 'checking and withholding the men of four of the five great provinces of Ireland, and not one foot have I gone back before any man in that time nor before a multitude of men, nor shall I retreat before Ferdia, Fergus. For as the rush bows down before the torrent in the middle of the stream, so will Ferdia bow before my sword, if once he shows himself here in combat with the Hound of Ulster.'

Then Fergus returned to where Maeve's army was encamped. And Ferdia, after the banqueting and the feasting and rejoicing were over, returned to his own quarters and told his own people what had happened and that he was bound to meet Cuchullain at the ford in the morning.

When they heard this his troops and servants were far from joy and merriment, in spite of the high spirits of Ferdia who was still half drunk, for they knew that wherever these two great heroes, these two battle-breakers and slayers of hundreds should meet in single combat, one or both of them must fall; and if it was only one who fell, well they knew that it would not be Cuchullain and that they would lose their own great chief, for it now seemed impossible to overthrow Cuchullain on his chosen ground at the ford.

Now during the early part of the night Ferdia slept heavily, being overcome with the liquor he had taken, but towards the middle of the night the sleep left him and his brain cleared and he woke and found that he could not sleep again. He remembered the combat that he had to fight in the morning, and anxiety and care began to worry him; partly it was fear of Cuchullain, but principally it was anger and sorrow that he had promised to fight him at the ford, his foster-brother; and fear of losing Finndabar particularly and Maeve's other great promises gnawed at him, and he began to get angry with himself and churlish towards Cuchullain because his feelings were complex and inexplicable, so he tossed about and could sleep no more.

Finally he rose in the cold, misty morning, and called his charioteer and said:

'Yoke my horses and come with me. I'll sleep better at the ford.'

But the charioteer began to rebuke him, saying:

'You'd be better off to stay where you are. I wish you would not go to meet Cuchullain at the ford.'

'Stay quiet,' said Ferdia, 'and harness the horses.' Ferdia was angry with himself in the dawn, and the more he thought of what had happened the angrier he became. 'There'll be no turning back,' he said, 'until the Hound's body lies reeking in the ford as offal for the croaking ravens above it.'

'It is not right for you to speak like that about your friend, Cuchullain,' said the charioteer, 'no credit to you for it.'

'Mind your own business,' said Ferdia, 'and get on with your work.'

And so, irritable and with uneasiness between them, they set out for the ford. When they got there Ferdia was overcome with a weariness and a certain kindness, and he said to his charioteer:

'Take the cushions and the skins out of the chariot like a good man, and spread them out for me on the bank till I see

83

would I get a little more sleep before the fighting.'

So the charioteer did as Ferdia asked and, as he lay down, Ferdia said to him:

'Take a look, lad, and see that Cuchullain is not coming.'

'He is not, I'm sure of it,' said the charioteer.

'Look again,' said Ferdia.

'Cuchullain is not such a little speck that we wouldn't see him if he was there,' said the lad.

'True enough,' said Ferdia, 'he's heard that I'm coming to meet him to-day and has decided to keep away.'

'Oh Ferdia,' said the charioteer, 'that is no way to be going on. It's not right to insult him and be disloyal to him in his absence. Don't you remember when you were fighting in the Eastern lands on the borders of the Tyrrhene sea and your sword was wrenched from your grasp; how you would have surely been killed but for Cuchullain rushing forward to recover it for you, killing all round him to get it for you? And do you not remember where we were that same night?'

'I do not,' Ferdia replied angrily.

'We were in the house of Scathach's steward,' said the lad, 'and you crossed words with that giant, half-witted pot boy there. And don't you remember how he struck you in the middle of the back with his great three pronged meat fork and hurled you through the door again? And that it was Cuchullain who rushed in and gave the fellow a blow of his sword that severed the top half of him from the bottom half, and if it was only for that alone, you should not discredit him.'

'What use is it to remind me of these things now,' said Ferdia in anguish. 'You had right to say them to me last night, and we would not be here at all. However, it's done now, and I'll try to sleep. You keep a good look out.'

'I'll watch,' said the charioteer, 'so that unless a man drop out of the clouds above to fight with you, none shall escape me.'

And saying this he sat beside Ferdia's head, while the warrior dropped into a deep and refreshing sleep.

And at about the same time, in the misty light of the early morning, Maeve, stretched on her couch beside Aillil, nudged him with her elbow and said in a hoarse, half-musing whisper:

'Provided that Cuchullain falls by Ferdia, it will be just as well if he's killed himself too; for it's certain that if he kills his friend, it is we ourselves he'll come after next.'

Meanwhile Cuchullain and his charioteer, Laeg, were talking together after Fergus had left them with the news that Ferdia was to come to the ford next morning.

'How do you intend to spend tonight,' asked Laeg when Fergus had gone.

'The same as every other night,' said Cuchullain, 'why?'

'Because,' said Laeg, 'it crossed my mind that Ferdia won't come to the ford alone to-morrow. For such a fight as this the hosts and chieftains of Ireland will assemble to look on and you may be sure that Ferdia will come to the combat washed and bathed and perfumed, with his hair freshly cut and scented and plaited and in all the great magnificence of a battle-champion. But you are worn out and tired after all these combats, unwashed and uncombed. And it seems to me that you would do yourself honour if you went home to Emer at Slieve Fuad for to-night, and let her attend to you, so that you might not appear dishevelled and ragged to-morrow before the men of Ireland.'

Cuchullain thought that there was sound sense in this advice and went back to Emer, who was gentle and loving to him after their separation from each other. Then, when it was full day, he returned to his camp. And he did this so that the men of Ireland would not say it was from fear or nervousness that he rose early to be at the ford. And, in the broad daylight, refreshed and comforted, he said to Laeg:

'Laeg, harness the horses and yoke our war-chariot and let us go now to the ford, for Ferdia was always an early rising champion and it would not do to keep him waiting.'

'The chariot is yoked and the horses are harnessed,' said Laeg, 'so mount it now, and it will not disgrace your courage or your skill.'

So Cuchullain sprang into the war-chariot and the battle-victorious and red-sworded hero grasped the hand-rail, and Laeg cracked his whip and with a leap and a pawing of the air, the two great steeds, the Grey of Macha and the Black Steed of the Glen, bounded forward. And up and around him rose the screeching and the wailing of the Bochanachs and the Bonawnachs, the spirits of the air and of battle, to strike terror and miserable fear into the souls of his enemies.

And as he came Ferdia's charioteer heard the roar of Cuchullain's approach; the clamour and the hissing and the tramp; and the thunder and the clatter and the scream; for he heard the discs for throwing clanking together as the chariot careered towards them; and he heard the tall spears hiss in the whipping wind, and the swords clash in their scabbards, and the helmet clang and the armour ring; and the arms sawed against one another and the javelins swung, and the ropes strained and the wheels of the chariot clattered; and the chariot creaked and the hooves of the horses thundered on the ground as that warrior and champion, Cuchullain, came forward to the ford, and approached him.

Then he woke Ferdia and said:

'Get up, Ferdia, for he is coming now... the Hound of Valour, a noble hawk of battle, the wind of combat in search of victory. A year ago I knew he would come, the hero of Emhain, the Hound of Ulster in his might.'

Then Ferdia sprang up in anger and said:

'For God's sake keep quiet, has he bribed you to praise him to me or what? He's late and I'm tired of waiting here to kill him, so let's get on with it.'

And soon Ferdia's charioteer looking across the ford saw a marvellous sight, Cuchullain's great, green canopied, battle chariot careering towards him with all the swiftness and power of Laeg and the mighty horses. Thin and well-seasoned was the body of it, lofty and long the spears that adorned it, that lithe war chariot. Under the yokes were two great-eared, savage and prancing steeds, bellied like whales and broad chested, they snorted and blew as they charged; high flanked and wide hooved, their pasterns fine, their loins broad and their spirits untamable, the long maned Grey of Macha and the tufted Black of the Glen. Like a hawk on a stormy day, like the gust of a gale on a March day across the plain; like a stag at the beginning of the chase, such was the pace of the two steeds, touching the soil as if it were on fire, so that the whole earth trembled and shook at the violence of their coming.

And as they travelled Cuchullain instructed Laeg that if he should grow weak in the fight, or seem to be giving way before Ferdia, he was to taunt him with cowardice and fling reproaches and bad names at him, so that his anger would rise and he would fight more bitterly than before. But if he were doing well then Laeg was to praise him to keep his spirits up.

And Laeg laughed and said:

'Is it like this you want me to taunt you: Come on Cuchullain, you're more like a child than a man, that Ferdia throws over as easily as a cat waves its tail? Or like a mother would play with her child?'

'That will do,' said Cuchullain laughing too, 'I should surely fight better after that.'

When they came to the ford Cuchullain drew up on the north side and Ferdia on the south side.

And Ferdia was still full of anger with himself and tried to justify it with sneers, so he said to Cuchullain:

'What brings you here, Cua?'

Now Cu means Hound and would have been a welcome indeed, but Cua means 'squint-eyed', and this was how Ferdia insulted Cuchullain. And Ferdia did this because he wanted to appear bold and unconcerned. So he said again:

'Welcome, squint eye.'

But Cuchullain answered seriously: 'Up to to-day no greeting would have been more welcome than one from you, Ferdia, but to-day I will not accept it. Indeed, it would be more suitable for me to welcome you than for you to welcome me, since it is you who have invaded my province and pillaged and burned all before you.'

'Ah, little Cuchullain,' said Ferdia, 'what in the world ever persuaded you to come to this fight at all as if you were my equal? Don't you remember how when we were with Scathach you were my attendant whose job it was to whet my spears and make my bed.'

'True enough,' said Cuchullain, 'because I was younger and smaller than you in those days, and it was the custom for juniors to do as much for seniors. But that is not the situation now. There is no champion in the entire world to whom I am not equal, or whom I would refuse to fight.'

And at that each reproached the other bitterly, renouncing their friendship. Each taunted the other that the days end would see him dead and headless, with his blood strewing the grass or washing away in the stream; but Ferdia was the most bitter. Then Cuchullain said:

'Oh, in days gone by,
Together you and I
Fought — 't was do or die —
Wherever Scathach taught.
You, of all who nearest
Are to me, and dearest;
Kinsman without peer, this
Doom your fate has brought.'

But Ferdia, indignant rage having laid hold of him, would not listen and taunted Cuchullain again.

Then Cuchullain said again: 'It was not right, Ferdia, for you to have come here because of the meddling of Maeve. I have killed many of her champions and you have been fooled like them and blinded with the promise of gifts. Do you really think that Finndabar loves you? You're not the first she was promised to, yes, or lay with, in order to be persuaded to come here. How could there be anger or enmity between us after all that we shared together. Remember the vow we made never to fight each other. I tell you there is not one in the world who could persuade me to fight you.'

Ferdia paused after this, and was moved by it, for he knew it was the truth that Cuchullain spoke. But he knew too that it was too late for him to turn back. But his chivalrous and noble nature got the better of him then, and he said:

'It is too late, Cuchullain, my true friend, there's no point in talking about the past and we had better get on with what we came for. Let us choose our weapons and begin. What arms shall we select to-day?'

'The choice of weapons is yours until to-night,' said Cuchullain, 'since you were first to reach the ford.'

'Well, then,' said Ferdia, 'do you remember the missiles that we learned to throw so well with Scathach?'

'I do indeed,' said Cuchullain.

'Very well,' said Ferdia, 'if you remember, let us use them now.'

Then they each took up their two great shields, thick and bossed and heavy for defence, to cover their bodies, and their eight small, razor edged discs to throw horizontally, and their eight light javelins, and their eight ivory handled bolts, and their eight little darts for the fight. Backwards and forwards between them flew the weapons, like bees winging on a sunny day, and there was no cast that they threw that did not hit. From early morning until midday they continued to hurl the weapons at each other until they were blunted on the faces of each other's shields. And so good was the aim behind each cast that not one of them missed, yet so skilful was the defence that not a drop of blood was drawn on either side.

'There's no point in fighting with these any longer,' said Ferdia, 'for it's not with them that either of us can win.'

'Very good,' said Cuchullain.

'What arms shall we use now?' asked Ferdia.

'The choice is still yours,' said Cuchullain.

'Then let's try our strong, hard spears with the flaxen throwing thongs,' replied Ferdia.

'Right,' said Cuchullain.

So they took their shields again, and the well-balanced throwing spears, and with these they attacked one another from the middle of the day until nightfall. And although the defence was as good as it had been in the morning, so good was the spear casting that each drew red blood from the other.

And at nightfall, they ceased and threw away their weapons into their charioteers hands and ran towards one another in the middle of the ford and each put his arms around the other and gave him three friendly kisses in remembrance of the past. That night their horses were stabled in the same paddock, and their charioteers warmed themselves at the same fire after they had made for their warriors beds of comfortable rushes and skins with pillows such as wounded men need. And the physicians and surgeons came to heal them and tend their wounds; and of every herb and remedy that was given to Cuchullain, he sent half across the ford to Ferdia so that no man among the hosts of Maeve could have it to say that if Ferdia fell it was because Cuchullain had a better means of healing than he. And of all the food and pleasant drink that the men of Maeve's camp sent to Ferdia, he sent half north across the ford to Cuchullain, for Cuchullain had few to attend to his wants, whereas all the people of Maeve's camp were ready to attend Ferdia.

And so, for that night they rested in peace; but early next morning they rose and met again at the ford.

And this day it was Cuchullain's right to choose the weapons for combat. 'Let us take our great, well-tempered, broad bladed lances then,' said Cuchullain, 'so that the close combat will bring a decision more quickly than the shooting of the light weapons of yesterday. And let us yoke our horses and chariots and fight from them to-day.'

So they took two, great, heavy shields across their shoulders and their broad-bladed lances and charged and wheeled and thrust and struck at one another from the grim light of early morning, to the bloody sinking of the western sun. And if it were customary for the birds of the air to pass through the bodies of men in their darting flight, then they could have passed through the bodies of these two that day through the wounds and the gaps they made in each other, and carried away pieces of their flesh into the clouds and the sky around them.

And by the evening both men and horses and their charioteers were spent and exhausted, and Cuchullain said:

'Let's stop now Ferdia, for our charioteers and our horses can do no more – we are not like giants from the sea who must be forever destroying each other without rest; let battle cease now, and let us be friends once again.'

'Very well,' said Ferdia, gratefully enough, 'if it is time to stop.'

And they threw their arms to their charioteers and ran to greet each other in the same manner as they did the previous night. The horses shared the same paddock that night as well, and again their charioteers shared the same fire after seeing to the warriors, for their injuries were so terrible that night that the physicians and surgeons could do little except try to staunch the flow of blood. And, as on the previous night, every remedy and salve that was given to Cuchullain, he sent half across to Ferdia and Ferdia in his turn sent to Cuchullain half of the food that was brought to him.

And they rested as well as they could that night, which was little because of their terrible wounds, and rose early the following morning and went again to the ford.

And that morning Cuchullain saw an evil look and a dark glowering look on Ferdia's face.

'Why are you so mean and evil looking to-day, Ferdia,' asked Cuchullain, 'and look at me in that vicious way?'

'Not from any fear of you,' snarled Ferdia, 'for there's no man in Ireland I couldn't kill to-day.'

'Oh Ferdia,' said Cuchullain in sorrow, 'it is a great tragedy for you to come and fight me, your friend and foster-brother, on the word of a woman. Not Finndabar's beauty, nor the coaxing of Maeve, nor all the wealth of the world would have brought me out to fight with you. Why don't you go back while you still can, for a fight to the death it must be between us if we go on, and I have not the heart to fight against you; my strength fails me when I think of the evil that has come between us; turn back, Ferdia, and no disgrace to you because of the false promises made to you by Maeve.'

'I can't, Cuchullain,' cried Ferdia, 'until one of us falls. I know what Maeve is and what her promises are worth, but for all that I cannot withdraw now. My honour at least, Cu, will be avenged, and I have no fear of death. Do not throw it in my face what I have done, my friend, but let us choose our arms, and fight as warriors and men.'

'If that is the way it must be,' said Cuchullain, 'that is the way it will be; what weapons shall we use?'

'Our heavy, two handed, smiting swords,' said Ferdia, 'for they will bring us into closer combat, and nearer to a conclusion, than our spears of yesterday.'

So they took two great, full length shields, and their great, double-edged swords, and all that day they hewed and hacked at each other; striking and trying to lay each other low; to cut and to slaughter and destroy each other until they struck masses and gobbets of flesh, larger than the head of a month old child, from the shoulders and thighs and shoulder blades of each other.

And the battle lasted without respite all that day until in the evening Ferdia cried:

'Let us cease now, Cuchullain.'

'Very well,' replied the other, 'if it is time.'

And they parted then, coldly, and threw their arms to their charioteers. And their horses did not share the same paddock that evening, nor did their charioteers sleep beside the same fire, but Laeg slept with his master on the north side of the ford and Ferdia's charioteer with him on the south side.

In the morning Ferdia rose early and went to the ford alone, for he knew well that the battle would be decided that day, and that on that day and in that place one or both of them would fall. And then he put on his full battle armour for the coming fight; the silken, gold embroidered trews and toughened leather kilt. And on his belly a great flagstone, shallow, of adamantine stone that he had brought from Africa; and over that the solid, twice molten iron skirt about his waist, through fear and dread of the Gae-Bolga on that day. And on his head his crested helmet, studded with forty glittering carabuncles and gleaming with enamel and crystal and rubies and gems from the east. Into his right hand he took his great, death-dealing spear and on his left side he hung his curved battle sword, razor-sharp, and golden hilted. Across his back he hung his massive battle shield, with fifty great bosses on it, each of which would reflect the image of a boar, and with its great central boss of red gold.

And then, when he was fully armed, he prepared himself for the coming battle by practising a great number of wonderful feats of arms; more than he had ever learned from Scathach, and which he had himself perfected in his years of war.

And when Cuchullain came to the ford he saw Ferdia practising there and said to Laeg:

'You see the wonderful feats that Ferdia is doing. They will all be turned on me to-day. Then do not forget what I told you; if I look like being bested you must taunt me and deride me to get my anger up.'

'I'll remember,' said Laeg.

Then Cuchullain put on his battle armour, and he in his turn practised many skills and feats he had perfected by himself and Ferdia watching knew that they would be tried on himself that day.

'What weapons will we use to-day?' asked Cuchullain.

'To-day the choice is yours,' replied Ferdia.

'Very well, then,' said Cuchullain, 'let us try the feat of the ford in which all weapons are allowed.'

'Very well,' replied Ferdia, but even as he said it he was full of sorrow, because he knew that Cuchullain had destroyed every champion and hero who ever fought the feat of the ford with him.

Terrible and mighty were the deeds done that day at the ford by the two mighty champions of Europe; the two great hands of the western world that bestowed gifts and pay and reward on men; the two pillars of the valour of the Gael; the two keys of bravery of the world, brought together in a fight to the death through the lies and trickery of Aillil and Maeve.

From the early morning they hurled their missiles at each other until noon, when their rage became wild and uncontrollable and they drew near one another in blind blood fury.

And then, suddenly, Cuchullain sprang from the bank of the ford and knocked Ferdia backwards and stood upon the boss of his shield, seeking to strike off his head from above with the rim of his own shield. But Ferdia gave his shield a thrust with his left elbow and cast Cuchullain from it like a bird, so that he came down again upon the bank. Again Cuchullain sprang before the other could get up and struck at Ferdia's head, but Ferdia gave his shield a thrust with his left knee and hurled Cuchullain back again.

And Laeg saw what was happening, and began to reproach Cuchullain as he had been told to do if he saw the warrior being bested:

'Ah, Cuchullain,' he shouted, 'this warrior throws you off like a whore throws away her child; as the river flings its foam; goes through you like an axe through a rotten tree, binds you as woodbine binds the tree; pounces on you like a hawk on a little bird, so that you can never be called a warrior again, you little twisted fairy, you.'

When Cuchullain heard these words he sprang again with the speed of the wind, the swiftness of the swallow, fiery as a dragon and powerful as the lion, and landed on the boss of Ferdia's shield and swung at his head. But Ferdia gave the shield a shake and tossed Cuchullain back as if he had never been there.

And then, for the first time, Cuchullain's great battle rage came on him. His countenance changed and he appeared to grow and swell so great was the rage that overcame him, until he seemed to tower as a terrible giant of the sea until he overtopped Ferdia.

So close was the struggle between them that their heads met above and their feet met below and their arms in the middle around the rims and bosses of their shields. So close was the struggle that their shields burst and split from their centres to their rims, and they turned and bent and twisted and shivered their spears from their points to their hafts. So

close were they locked that the Bochanachs and the Banaw-
nachs and the demons of war screamed from the rims of their
shields and the hilts of their swords and the hafts of their
spears. So closely were they locked together that the river was
cast out of its bed and dried up beneath them so that a couch
could be made in the middle of its course for a king or a queen
without a drop of liquid falling on them, except what sprang
from the two champions, as they trampled and hewed at each
other in the middle of the ford.

Such was the terror of the fight that the horses of the Gael
in fear and madness, rushed away wildly, bursting their yokes
and their chains and their tethers and their traces; and the
women and the children and the weak and the camp followers
among Maeve's hosts fled away southwestwards out of the
camp.

Just at that moment Ferdia caught Cuchullain in an un-
guarded instant and plunged his short-edged sword into his
breast, so that Cuchullain's blood streamed to his girdle and
the wet soil of the bottom of the ford was streaked and crim-
soned with his blood. And Ferdia, seeing his advantage,
rained blow after blow on Cuchullain who could barely defend
himself against the fierce, slashing, hurricane of blows that
Ferdia rained on him – even ignoring his own defence – in a
frenzied attempt to finish the Hound.

Then Cuchullain, unable to withstand this onslaught, called
to Laeg to pass him the Gae-Bolga.

Now the manner of using the Gae-Bolga, a Scythian weapon,
was to hurl it with the foot at your enemy. It made the wound
of one spear on entering a person's body, but it had thirty
barbs to open behind and it could not be cut out of a man's
body until he was cut open.

When he heard Cuchullain, Laeg sent the Gae-Bolga floating
down the stream and Cuchullain caught it in the fork of his
foot.

Now, when Ferdia heard Cuchullain call for the Gae-Bolga,
he made a downward stroke of his shield to protect his body
and Cuchullain, seeing his opportunity, rammed a short spear
with the palm of his hand over the edge of Ferdia's shield and
above the edge of his armour so that it pierced him through
and emerged the other side. Then, Ferdia gave an upward
thrust of his shield to protect his upper body, though it

was help that came too late, and Cuchullain threw the Gae-Bolga as forcibly as he could cast it underneath at Ferdia, so that it broke through the iron-linked skirt, and broke in three parts the adamantine stone, and cut its way into his body so that every crevice and cavity in him was filled with its barbs.

'Ah!' Ferdia groaned, 'that's the end. But it is not right that it should be by your foot I fell and not your hand.'

Then Cuchullain ran to Ferdia and, lifting him in spite of all his great armour, carried him to the northern bank of the ford in order that he might die on that side and not on the other with the army of Maeve.

And, when he lay him down, a great weakness came over Cuchullain himself and he collapsed beside the body of Ferdia.

But Laeg, who could see the danger, roused him again.

'Cuchullain, Cuchullain,' he cried, splashing water in the warrior's face, 'rise up from there or we are dead men. The army of Connacht is on the move towards us and it is not single combat they'll give us when they reach us, since you have killed Ferdia.'

'What does it matter, now that I've killed my greatest friend,' asked Cuchullain,'... oh Ferdia,' he added, addressing the body of his comrade, 'it was great treachery and desertion of the men of Ireland to bring you to fight here with me, knowing that one of us must die. Oh Ferdia, you are the greatest loss to Ireland; I wish to God it was me who lay there instead of you.'

'Ah,' said Laeg, 'stop that. It is true enough that if he had his way it is you who would be there now. Now hurry, before they come and slaughter us.'

But Cuchullain paid no attention. For a long while he remained silent, bending alone above the body of his friend in great grief. Then he stood up and turned away and, without looking at Ferdia's body, said to Laeg:

'Laeg, remove his armour and let me see that golden brooch which cost him his life here to-day.'

Then Laeg took off Ferdia's horny armour and took the brooch from the mantle beneath, and handed it to Cuchullain. Cuchullain looked at it lying in his palm, and tears, such as only a strong warrior can weep, poured from his eyes and fell on that ancient brooch.

'Laeg,' he said, without looking up, for indeed if he had

looked up he could not have seen, 'Laeg, now cut open the body and take out the Gae-Bolga.'

So Laeg did so and when he drew out the spear, all red with the blood of Ferdia still on it, Cuchullain lamented over his friend 'to whom I have served a draught of blood', and said:

'Now we will go, for every other combat that I ever fought or will fight seems like a game to me compared with this battle with Ferdia, this pillar of gold that I have overthrown.' And as he left he made this lament:

> 'Wars were shared and gay for each
> Until Ferdia faced the breach;
> Together we had shared the skill
> Of Scathach, who had taught us well.
> Equal was the praise she gave;
> Equal was her praise to each.
>
> Wars were shared and gay for each
> Until Ferdia faced the breach,
> Well loved pillar of pure gold
> Lying now beside the ford, dead; cold!
> Who, when on his foes he fell,
> Killed as far as eye could reach.
>
> Wars were shared and gay for each
> Until Ferdia faced the breach;
> Lion fiery, fierce and bright,
> Wave whose might nothing withstands,
> Sweeping with the shrinking sands,
> Destruction on the beach.
>
> Wars were shared and gay for each
> Until Ferdia faced the breach;
> Gentle Ferdia; dear to me,
> Always shall his image be –
> Yesterday a mountain looming,
> Now a shadow in the gloaming.'

Deirdre and the Sons of Usna

CHAPTER ONE

Conor Mac Nessa became king of Ulster by a trick. When he
was a youngster his mother, a widow called Ness, was ambi-
tious and beautiful. Now she was not highborn enough to consider that Conor could ever become king and the thought
never entered the minds of those who knew them, because the
king at the time was Fergus Mac Ri, a powerful and noble
man whom his people loved. Although Ness knew that Conor
was not in line for the throne, she was of sufficient rank to
mingle at Court and she set out deliberately to attract Fergus,
which she did so successfully that he developed a considerable
passion for her. But she would not give in to him when he
asked her to marry him, and played with him and tantalised
him until he was ready to accede to any request.

Then she made it a condition of her marrying Fergus that,
for one year, he would leave the sovereignty and that Conor
should take his place: 'so that she could have it said that her
son sat on the throne and that his children should be called
the descendants of a king.'

Fergus didn't like the idea, and his people liked it even less,
but she absolutely refused to marry him unless he agreed, so
at last he did so and resigned the kingdom to Conor. But as
soon as Conor sat on the throne Ness set out to win the hearts
and allegiance of the people from Fergus and transfer them
to Conor. And she was so successful in this that when Fergus
demanded the kingship back he found that there was a league
of chiefs and nobles against him who had been won over by
her bribes and favours, and the league was so strong that he
could do nothing. They said that they liked Conor, who had
become their friend and protector, and they were not disposed
to part with him; and furthermore that Fergus had abandoned
the kingdom for a year only to gain a wife and therefore cared
little for it and didn't deserve to get it back, and, while agree-

ing that he was entitled to keep his wife if he wished, they insisted that the kingship should pass to Conor.

Fergus was so enraged at this that he, together with his followers, left Ulster – leaving his wife behind – and went into Connacht where he found refuge with Maeve and Aillil.

But he swore to be revenged on Conor and that is how he came to fight with Maeve and Aillil against Ulster in the Tain Bo Cuailgne when Cuchullain defended Ulster at the ford against the champions of Maeve's army.

But, as the years passed away, the memory of their old quarrels died too between Fergus and Conor, and Fergus yearned with a terrible homesickness to be back in Ulster. So at length he returned to Ulster with his followers and Conor did him great honour and placed him next to himself in the land. But all the time he watched him with great jealousy, for Conor was getting old and bitter and the knowledge that he sat in Fergus's rightful seat was with him always and he knew that many of the older chiefs would like to see Fergus resume the throne even after all that time.

If he dared he would have shut Fergus up in his foulest dungeon or have had him killed outright, but he knew that this would be disastrous to himself for the men of Ulster would not have stood for it. And so, year by year, suspicion and hatred grew in him so that some men feared and dreaded him and few felt for him the affection and reverence that is due a true king.

Yet for the younger chiefs, who knew nothing of what had passed between Conor and Fergus years before, or who learned it only as history that happened before they were born, the reign of the gigantic Fergus and his mightly deeds were hearsay; old wives tales told by toothless men and to be taken with a sceptical smile and a fistful of salt. And though they looked on the giant hero with interest and considerable awe, he seemed more like an ancient demigod, than a human being like themselves, who had somehow lingered on from an historic past.

At this time Ulster was at peace and instead of the grim aura of war, days of laughter and sunshine filled the lives of the people; the corn ripened and was harvested; the cattle fattened; the gold and precio s metals were worked and trade prospered. The young men contended on the playing field instead of among the carnage of the battlefield, and the young women grew up with the expectation of marriage before them. And it became the custom, as in earlier times, for each chief in his turn to provide a great banquet for the king and his followers and in due course it became the turn of Felim, chief of Conor's story-tellers, to prepare such a feast.

For a year he had been in preparation. He had a great, immense hall built close to his own castle, big enough to accommodate the king's retinue and his own guests. Oak trees by the hundred had been felled and trimmed for the beams of the walls and the ceiling, which had been laced and latticed with wattle and then sealed with clay. Outside the doorways and the lintels were of marble stone, and the flags of black basalt. And all around the banqueting hall were also built sleeping quarters for those guests who could not be accommodated in the castle, kitchens and stables for the horses. From the surrounding countryside butter and cream, cheese and curds, cakes and bread; cattle, sheep and swine for the table were brought in in preparation, and fruit and vegetables from Ireland and across the seas were stored, together with great quantities of honey and ale, mead and the wine of Greece and Rome. Musicians, dancers, men and women; those who played the harp and the lute, from foreign lands with strange uncouth romances, and from Ireland with the stories of the ancients; all were there and in readiness for the great feast, about which, Felim swore, the men of Ireland would talk for many years to come. And about that he was right, but not for the reason which he anticipated.

On the day appointed Conor set out in state from Emhain Macha, which was his seat of state, with all the champions of the Red Branch Knights in attendance. It was a glorious day in which the sun wheeled overhead like a great chariot of fire in a blue plain, and below the splendour of the king all but matched its own. For as he left the great gate of Emhain Macha and turned his face eastward on the road to Felim's country, a great emblazoned banner spanned the highway like an arch. A hundred knights in scarlet cloaks embroidered in gold and riding black horses pranced at the head of the column; then a hundred more in emerald green on white horses; then yet another hundred in deep blue cloaks with silver fringes riding chestnut steeds, and then five hundred of the knights in saffron yellow cloaks, tall and proud, in chariots of beaten bronze drawn by well matched pairs and driven by charioteers in white tunics appeared, the scythes and armour of the chariots flashing in the sun. But the scythes were folded up from the axles of the war-chariots, and there was grandeur in the sight without an element of war or foreboding.

The king in all his glory came next. And from where he sat in the large open, four-wheeled chariot that carried him, with its canopy of purple, he could see the glitter and the twinkle of the sun on the helmets and spear points of the knights who rode before him. More knights followed, and then the remainder of his retinue which was upwards of a thousand people. But in spite of the sunshine and the glorious panoply, the mouth of the king rarely smiled and his watching eyes seldom stopped moving, as he himself seldom relaxed in comfort.

Slowly the cavalcade moved along the highway under the sun, but as the afternoon wore on some dark-centred clouds blew up from the east and more followed until, like a curtain drawn by a cord from the west, a grey cloud came between them and the sun; and before night fell a wind followed and raised high clouds of choking dust that hung around them and filled their eyes, their ears and their mouths with grime and settled on everything.

Then, just as they reached the castle of Felim, the storm broke with a huge crash of thunder and a flash of brilliant light that showed the place for a moment in a blue-white light, and then shut it out again as suddenly as the rain emptied from the sundered clouds above.

Felim stood at the door of the banqueting hall, framed by the light from inside, and his cloak billowed and flapped behind him in the wind as he went forward to welcome his royal guest.

'Welcome, Conor,' he cried, 'come in out of this terrible night and lets have music and a song – and a drink for Conor.' But his excitement and goodwill were no use; indeed his evening looked like being completely spoiled, for the king sat there and glowered, scarcely bothering to speak to anyone, while the storm roared and thundered outside; such a storm as no one could remember before.

The king took this as an omen. 'This is no common storm,' he muttered, 'I have the feeling that some catastrophe will fall on us after this night.'

But Felim continued to try and cheer him up and make his banquet a success, though he was fighting a losing battle. However, after the guests had been washed and warmed and given drink, they sat at the enormous tables groaning with the food, and the banquet began.

But the king had hardly raised the first bite to his mouth when a dreadful scream came from the palace.

'What is that,' asked the king, his face going pale.

And Felim, cursing the impulsive night three quarters of a year ago, said: 'It is nothing, Conor; my wife, she is in labour.'

'That didn't sound like the scream of any woman to me,' said the king. 'Bring her here till we see for ourselves, if she is able.'

So messengers went and brought Felim's wife into the banqueting hall, and sure enough she confirmed that it was not she who had screamed, but the child itself who had screamed in the womb even before it was born. Then Catha, the king's druid, stood up and put his hand on her and said:

'Aye, indeed! It is a girl-child who is here, and her name will be Deirdre – which is alarm – and she will be well-named because she will bring evil and woe and war to Ulster with her.'

Then, when Catha had said this, the woman left again for her bed, and the entire company returned to the banquet, but without an appetite for it. The king was deep in thought, and no one had the courage to interrupt him.

Then, after a little while, a messenger came to say that Felim's wife had given birth, and it was indeed a girl who had been born.

'Let her be killed,' cried the knights, afraid of the prophesy.

'No,' said the king, in a perverse humour. 'We will not commit an evil deed to avoid the course of a prophesy.' Though, indeed, it was no fear of doing evil that prevented him, or had ever prevented him in the past. 'Let Catha go out,' he said, 'and consult the stars to discover her destiny. We owe our host no less than that, and may the future be good and prosperous for him and his family.'

So Catha went out into the night, where the storm had passed, leaving dark clouds behind racing across the face of the night to catch it up, and stood in the ramparts of the castle trying to read the stars. He studied the moon and from his robes took out his tablets and runes and studied them, and performed several other mystic rites which would help him. He did everything with great care, because he knew that what would be revealed was of the utmost importance to Ulster, and when he knew it all he was startled.

He was gone a long time and meanwhile those in the banqueting hall had been celebrating, following the king's lead, the birth of the child and all the earlier ominous atmosphere was gone. Now all were merry and the place rang with noise and laughter and Felim in particular was delighted at the turn things had taken, for the king was in great spirits. But when Catha stood in the doorway, silently looking at them with a strange look, silence ran down the length of the room like a wind rippling across a cornfield. The laughter stopped, and everyone turned to look at Catha. The King's eyes were fastened on him, almost hypnotically, for an instant and then, with a sudden movement, he laughed too loudly and said:

'Well, we hope the omens prophesy good luck, and no harm to her parents.' And he drank a toast to her with a flamboyant gesture. But even as the drink passed down his throat the laugh flew out of his mouth and fear gripped his chest making it difficult for him to swallow. He nearly choked on the draught, but turned his eyes, expectantly and challengingly, on Catha.

Catha returned his look gravely. 'Not to her parents, but to the province and its king and chiefs will this child bring misfortune,' he said. 'She will be so beautiful that queens will be jealous of her and kings go to war for her. Beware, Conor, she is born for misfortune to Ulster and the downfall of the Red Branch Knights.'

Then, again, the knights and nobles sprang up and together shouted that if such evil were going to follow her, then it would be better to kill her while she was still an infant.

But Conor quietened them, out of perversity or what strange motive it is hard to say.

'Let us see this harbinger of bad luck,' he said. 'Bring in the child.'

So the tiny infant was brought in, straight from its birthplace, and when it felt the warmth and the lights and the sounds about her, she, marvellous to relate, puckered up her face and crowed and smiled up at the stern king.

At this he was moved to gentleness. He reached out and took the baby from the nurses arms and stood with her for a moment. Then, loudly, he addressed the company.

'The prophecies and omens of the seers I believe and honour, but I do not believe that any good can come out of killing this child. Therefore I will make at least one part of his cold prophecy come true, for I will take her as my wife when she comes of marriageable age, and so she shall be a queen. I shall place her under my special protection now and make myself responsible for her. She shall be reared by me in a secret place and any who lifts his hand against her must reckon with the king himself. In that way I will be better able to guard against the prophecy.'

And the knights did not raise a protest, though they were not satisfied with the way things turned out. When they said nothing Catha said:

'Conor, you will live to regret this, but, since it is your will that she must live then she will be a child of sorrow, and Deirdre of the Sorrows will be her name.'

'It is a nice name,' said Conor, 'I like Deirdre. And when she is old enough to foster with a nurse, let her be brought to me.'

As soon as she was old enough Conor took the child away from her parents and had her brought up by a nurse called Leabharcam, a wise and skilful nurse, who reared her in one of Conor's hidden fortresses deep in a wood private to the king. The fortress had a lovely garden around it surrounded by a high wall where no man could see her, and outside the wall was a deep moat. Savage wolf hounds guarded the place at night, and Conor was satisfied that Deirdre was secure there; secure from the fate foretold by Catha, who was the only one allowed to visit her other than himself, and secure for himself when she matured in his old age.

And for years Deirdre grew there with Leabharcam her teacher and Catha and the king as her visitors, and they were the only men she knew. But she was not unhappy, for Leabharcam loved her very much and taught her all that she knew; the secrets of living things, birds that fly and beasts that run; she taught her about plants and roots and their names and uses, both of them and of their fruits. And Leabharcam taught her the motion of the stars and the planets so that she understood time and the changes of the seasons. Deirdre grew tall and lissome and beautiful; more beautiful than any maiden of the world; beautiful of body and of mind. And as she grew older and more womanly beautiful, so did the ageing king's visists become more numerous.

Then, one winter's day when the snow lay over the garden in smooth layers and hung upon the dark branches of the bare trees like livid fruits, Deirdre was standing at a window looking out at where Catha had killed a calf so that she might have veal for her meal

And suddenly she sighed. Now Leabharcam hearing the sigh, a thing she had never known Deirdre to do before, turned to her and said:

'What ails you, child?'

'I don't know, Leabhar,' said Deirdre, who used this affectionate name – which means book – because of her fondness for Leabharcam and because of her nurse's wisdom – 'I don't know,' she said, 'I feel sad.'

'Sad,' said Leabharcam, who had lived in fear that the day would come when Deirdre might say that, for she knew what it meant, 'for what?'

'And lonely,' said Deirdre.

And Leabharcam knew that this was worse.

'Lonely?' she said.

'Yes,' said Deirdre.

'But how could you be lonely, child dear, with me here and the king and Catha to visit you?'

'Oh Leabhar,' said Deirdre, 'I don't know. I mean I do know, but don't misunderstand me when I say it. I'm lonely for youth... you – you are all so old.'

'Hush, child,' said Leabharcam, 'you must not say that the king is old, and he's coming to visit you to-day.' And she looked round nervously in case he had already arrived, for he was a silent man.

'But he *is* old,' said Deirdre, 'and I would dearly love to meet someone who is not; a young man. A young man with those three colours,' she said, pointing to where a raven stood in the snow dipping its beak in the blood of the calf: 'hair as black as the raven; cheeks as red as blood and his body as white as the snow.'

'Oh,' cried Leabharcam in terror, 'whisht child, and don't let the king hear you or he would kill him for sure.'

'Kill who?' asked Deirdre immediately.

'Never mind who,' snapped Leabharcam, angry at her mistake, 'there's only one who is the like of that.'

But Deirdre wasn't listening to her.

'Last night,' said Deirdre, 'I saw him in a dream...'

'The gods between us and all harm,' said Leabharcam, 'you did not!'

'I did,' said Deirdre, 'and it is him I would marry and not the king. The king is old and grey and his face is ugly, and I think he is cruel too.'

'Hush child,' said Leabharcam, seriously worried, 'for if the king heard you talk like that Naisi's life wouldn't be worth that' and she snapped her crooked fingers with a crack.

'Naisi,' said Deirdre, 'who's he.'

'The man you have just described to me,' said Leabharcam drily, but with pity and understanding too, for she had been in love once herself, 'though how it is you could do it I don't pretend to know.'

'Naisi,' said Deirdre, 'Naisi?'

CHAPTER TWO

Now Naisi and his brothers Ainle and Ardan, the three sons of Usna, were the best loved of the Red Branch Knights; gracious and gentle in peace, skilful and swift-footed in the hunt, and brave and powerful in battle. And of the three Naisi was foremost of all Ulster's young chiefs. He was also an accomplished musician and he loved to wander abroad by himself with his small harp and sit somewhere and make music, to which he would put a song about what he saw, or what he thought or what he felt, or remembered.

One day he had gone out with his harp and was sitting under a beech tree on a hillock playing and singing just like this, his strong, aquiline face with the long dark hair thrown back, and the notes issuing from his white throat in competition with the birds.

It was springtime and the time for Deirdre's marriage with the king was approaching. And the closer it came the more restless and uneasy she had become until at last she was unable to stand being confined any longer and she persuaded Leabharcam to allow her to go for walks outside the limits of the fortress and the garden, where she could feel free, if only for a time. At first, from fear of what Conor might do if he found out, Leabharcam refused, but as Deirdre's distress increased, and she seemed to become really ill, Leabharcam at last agreed, and, secretly, Deirdre would go out in the morning or afternoon when the king wasn't expected and walk abroad in the world she knew little about.

And on one such day, when she had wandered to the edge of the wood where the sunlight on the grass was broken into brocaded strips by the leafy branches, she stopped when she heard music and the voice of a man making a song.

Now it is said that when Naisi made music the cows who heard it gave two thirds more milk – and it may be true, for farmers to-day are milking to music for that very reason – and any man or woman who heard him sing forgot their troubles while they listened and were filled with joy. And it was just like that with Deirdre; she was filled with joy.

She walked towards the music and, as soon as she saw who it was who sang, she recognised Naisi, though she had never set eyes on him before. And she went, at once shyly and impelled beyond herself, to pass him, but with her eyes down. And as she went past him, Naisi, seeing her beauty, couldn't help but remark on it because he had never seen her before, in Emhain or anywhere else; and he knew very well that a girl as beautiful as this wouldn't stay away from Emhain for very long unless there was a reason for it.

'Oh,' he cried, 'how beautiful...' and then, mischievously: 'How fair the doe that springs past me.'

But Deirdre answered him seriously: 'It is easy for doe's to be gentle and fair where there are no bucks.'

Then Naisi recognized her from the stories he had heard, and he was circumspect in his answer:

'You have your buck,' he said, 'the buck of the whole province of Ulster, king Conor himself.'

'But I don't love him,' she said, 'he's old and ugly, and if I were to choose, I would choose a young buck like yourself.'

And she looked straight at him. Now this was not brazenness on her part, but she spoke with her heart and with truth.

'You are the king's,' said Naisi.

'You say that only to avoid me,' said Deirdre.

'No,' replied Naisi, 'but because of the prophecy of Catha.'

Then Deirdre pulled a briar of wild roses and flung it at his head, saying: 'You are disgraced now if you reject me.'

'Please,' said Naisi, 'Deirdre, I love you too, but...'

She went up to him, half laughing, half crying; and in anger too and took both his ears in her hands.

'Two ears of mockery and shame you'll have,' she said shaking his head, 'if you leave me.'

He grinned at her then.

'Let me go... wife!' he said, and she let him go and they put their arms around one another.

Then Naisi said no more, but picked up his harp again and composed another song straight out of his heart and it was the sweetest, and the saddest; the most moving, the most joyous that he ever made. And Deirdre sat beside him until his brothers Ainle and Ardan came through the wood looking for Naisi.

They were horrified when they heard who Deirdre was and that Naisi intended to take her with him, and tried to dissuade him. But he was adamant, for he had given her all his love; all his stored knowledge and memories, all that he was and all that he knew. He told his brothers and, when they saw how it was between them, they said no more. Then Deirdre gave Naisi three kisses, and to his brothers each a kiss, and Naisi put her on his shoulder and together the four of them went through the wood.

They spent that night at Naisi's father's castle and, next day with their entire following – a hundred and fifty men, a hundred and fifty women, and the same number of hounds and servants, they left Ulster, but not before Naisi and Deirdre were married.

For several months they went from place to place, serving with this king or that; in Assaroe, near Ballyshannon, to Ben Eadair near Howth; from north to south and from east to west, and all the time Conor sought revenge and tried to kill them, either by ambush or by war, and always they escaped.

Because, apart from the prophecy and the fact that she was

under his protection which had been flouted, as Deirdre grew into a beautiful young woman and in spite of the fact that he was surrounded in his court with the choice women of the land, Conor had grown a passion for Deirdre who was lovelier than anything that he had seen or dreamed of; and he had nursed his passion jealously and kept it for his old age and his marriage with Deirdre which was to have taken place a few weeks after she ran away with Naisi.

And so he harrassed and harried the sons of Usna; plotted and planned for their destruction with a bitterness and vengeance that consumed his life from the moment he learned that Deirdre was gone; consumed his life, and grew in him as it consumed it.

And so Naisi, when he found no resting place in Ireland where he was driven and always driven by the men of Ulster, determined to leave the country and go to Alba – Scotland – where he landed with his followers, drove the wild inhabitants from the place, and carved out for himself a kingdom which had its seat in Glen Etive. And there he ruled with Deirdre and his brothers and became a powerful prince who loved his queen, Deirdre, with an immensity of love that grew and multiplied with the experience of each day.

They lived there in great happiness and contentment for many years. Sometimes Naisi and his followers warred with the native Picts, but more often they were at peace with their neighbours and with themselves.

But all the time king Conor's bitterness and lust for revenge grew, for old though he was, with sons in middle age, he burned for the lovely Deirdre; she had become an obsession with him and, at the moment when he was about to achieve it, she was whipped away from him. Now only one thought was in his mind; revenge. But try as he would he could think of no way of achieving it. There was no point in sending a man, or a group of men, to assassinate his enemies, even if he could find the knights willing to do it, for Naisi had a strong camp in Glen Etive, and short of a full-scale invasion there didn't seem a solution. An invasion Conor wasn't prepared for; his people would not stand for an undertaking of that magnitude for such a little cause and might – as he very well knew with his own example and that of Fergus before him – depose him for another if he pressed the point.

But, as these things so often happen, the answer came to him one evening at a mighty festival at Emhain Macha, when all the greatest lords and nobles in Ulster were assembled.

Conor sat at the head of the enormous principal table, with Fergus, old now but still vigorous, at his right hand; on the other side sat the mighty warrior Conall Cearnach and completing the awe-inspiring foursome at the top of the table was Cuchullain, still young, but of a terrible, fate-filled, brooding aspect:-

> Beside Conall as of old
> Sat Cuchullain, sombre, cold.
> For though his youth lay on his shoulder
> His deep eye was cold, and older;
> And in a red gloom round his head
> A dark raven of the dead
> Sang slowly songs of doom;
> All who looked at him and saw
> Felt their thoughts grow great with awe
> For his tragedy loomed loudly by his head.
> Like a god he sat before them
> Never seeing those about him
> And all men when they saw him went in dread.

Conor looked round the tremendous hall, whose farthest depths he could not distinguish from where he sat, though he knew that it was thronged with knights and retainers. Nearer, close to the seats of the three heroes and himself, there were three empty seats that he could see very well. They were at the places of the three sons of Usna which had remained like that ever since they went. And none ever remarked on it for it was known that the king had commanded that no one should speak of the sons of Usna in his presence. And it was while he looked broodingly at these three empty places that the means of getting his revenge occurred to Conor.

Slowly he glanced up from beneath his brows, his hard eyes beginning to light with excitement that he made an effort to conceal.

Gradually the scowl vanished from his face and he began to be merry; he laughed and made jokes and pressed more food and drink on the knights and his guests, and when the banquet was at its height, he raised his kingly voice and cried:

'Well, oh nobles and chiefs of Ulster, and Knights of the Red Branch, I would have you tell me something... in all your travels among the countries of the world have you ever seen a court more royal or a banquet more satisfying?'

'Never,' they roared.

'Is there anything lacking?' shouted Conor back at them.

'Nothing,' they roared again.

'But there is,' shouted Conor, silencing them. 'The Three Lights of Valour of the Gael, as we know them; the three sons of Usna.'

For a moment there was a great silence. Then Conor continued:

'It is a pity that for the sake of a woman they are not here with us.'

Then there was a tumult.

'Had we dared to say that, Conor,' they cried, 'we would have had them home long ago. Had we the three sons of Usna back again, all Ireland would give way before Ulster, so great is their strength.'

'I didn't know,' said Conor, 'that you wanted them back, but if that is your wish, let us send a messenger to Glen Etive to bring them home.'

There was another silence then; for the nobles realised that there was hardly a man among them whose word the sons of Usna would trust after the way in which they had been hounded.

'And whose word would they trust,' asked a voice.

Conor smiled craftily to himself, but it did not show on his face.

'I understand,' he said, 'that of all my nobles there are only three whose word the sons of Usna would accept; and they are Fergus, or Conall Cearnach or Cuchullain himself.'

'Then let them go,' cried the knights, 'and bring us back the Three Lights of Valour of the Gael.'

This was according to Conor's plan. Later that evening, when the banqueting was nearly done, and stories and music and drinking were being followed in groups around the fires and in the corners of the hall, Conor took Conall Cearnach aside into an ante-room.

He had already prepared his speech. He ushered Conall to a

seat beside him on a cushioned couch and, leaning forward in the gloom, for the ante-room was lit only with a rush-wick lamp, he said:

'Conall, you heard what happened at the banquet to-night. Much to my surprise, it seems the men of Ulster want the sons of Usna home again. I, of course, would like nothing better. And you know that you, or Fergus or Cuchullain must be the ones to bring them back. But a thought occurs to me. Suppose, by any chance that they did come back under your protection and safeguard, and that something should happen to them. They were killed, for example, through some mischance, then what would happen?'

Conall looked back at the king levelly, and said:

'If such a *mischance*,' and he stressed the word slightly, 'should happen while they were under my protection, not only him whose hand was stained, but every man in Ulster who had done them harm would feel my vengeance.'

Conor sighed and frowned.

'I was afraid you'd say that,' he replied. 'You are a man of great loyalty, Conall. But it is misguided. I had a good reason for asking you that question. To find out if your loyalty was to me, or to anyone else.'

Conall Cearnach said nothing. He stood up, looked at Conor, bowed a little stiffly, and stalked out quivering with anger.

Conor next had Cuchullain summoned. But when he saw the young man with the countenance of a tormented god standing before him, even Conor's cruel purpose faltered.

He asked his question falteringly and without looking Cuchullain in the face.

Cuchullain remained standing while the king spoke. Then quietly and without expression; almost without inflexion, he said:

'Conor, if any harm came to the sons of Usna while they were under my protection, not all the riches of the eastern world would keep your head on your shoulders in lieu of theirs.' And without saying another word he turned and walked away, leaving Conor, shaken, behind him.

Then Conor sent for Fergus.

It was on Fergus that he knew he must rely, so, while he was waiting, he thought about what he would say to him. When Fergus came in Conor greeted him warmly and threw an arm around his shoulder, and said, as if he were speaking to a life-long comrade and friend:

'Fergus there's a problem about the sons of Usna that just occurred to me; supposing any harm did come to them while they're here, what then?'

'What do you mean?' asked Fergus.

'Well, what would you do, for example,' asked Conor, 'it's not unforeseeable you know.'

Now Fergus didn't know how to reply. For one thing Conor's question had been so veiled that there was no indication of anything behind it; and even if there had been, Fergus's own position was such that he might not have seen it. For it was only recently that he had come back to Ulster, to die really, and he had been set high in honour and position by Conor; to bring back the sons of Usna would raise his prestige even higher, particularly among the nobles and people of the province, and might mean the return of the throne, if not to him, at least to his children. And so, after a long silence in which he considered all these things, and while Conor watched him closely, he replied:

'If any Ulsterman harmed them, Conor, I'd avenge the hurt. But I don't anticipate that any hurt would come to them while they came under the protection of your sovereign word.'

'Nor,' said Conor opening his eyes and spreading his hands wide, 'do I. But it could happen. And if it did...?'

'If it did,' said Fergus darkly, 'then I'd have revenge.'

'On whom?'

'On whoever did it, of course,' replied Fergus.

'And what about my position?'

'Your position?'

'Yes. Would you have revenge on me too?'

'Why should I,' replied Fergus, 'for I know well that you would not harm them when they come under the seal of your word.'

'Therefore you would not turn your sword against me; I knew I could trust you Fergus, you are a loyal man, and a true king. Therefore to-morrow let you go and bring the king's message to the sons of Usna, and say that he longs to welcome them, and tell them eat no meat until they reach the feast I will have prepared for them here at Emhain.'

And so, on the following day, Fergus with his sons Illan the

Fair and Buinne the Red, together with Fergus's shield-bearer Caillan, sailed from Dun Borrach for Glen Etive.

But they had hardly sailed out of the harbour, where Conor had come to see them off with every appearance of goodwill, when he began to put his plan into effect. He turned and rode towards the fort of Borrach which dominated the harbour; Borrach, who was the local chief, by his side.

'I believe,' said Conor, 'that you are preparing a feast for me.'

'That is so, Conor,' replied Borrach, 'and right glad I am to be able to do it.'

'Well,' said Conor, 'it is a great hardship to me to think of disappointing you, but I shall reward you in other ways. Affairs of State confine me to Emhain at the moment, but Fergus Mac Ri stands beside me in power in Ulster and I would have you accept him in my place. When he returns from Alba invite him in my stead, and I will hold the honour paid to him as paid to me.'

'He will feast with me for three days,' said Borrach, 'for we are brothers of the Red Branch and he is under vow not to refuse the hospitality of any man when it is offered to him.'

Conor smiled again to himself when he heard this, which he already knew; for, in common with the other knights of the Red Branch, Fergus had made pledges which would bind him for life when he took his knighthood. These vows they made in the presence of kings and nobles and they dared not violate them, for whoever did so was utterly dishonoured; and one of Fergus's vows was that he would never refuse such an invitation.

Furthermore Conor knew that he would not refuse to accept the banquet at which he represented the king. But he had also laid it on Fergus to bring the sons of Usna to Emhain, knowing that they, too, were bound to come without delay when summoned by the king. And so he intended to separate the sons of Usna from their protector, and get them in his power.

Meanwhile Fergus's ship sailed north east from Ireland, through the rough passage of the North channel between the two countries, and onward until he sighted the coast of Argyle and turned towards Loch Etive. As his ship sailed up the calm loch, bordered by the rounded shoulders of heather-covered hills, the rippling water brown near the boat but blue and silver where it reflected the sunlight and the sky, Fergus stood in the prow and raised a great hunting cry.

Deirdre and Naisi were sitting in the sun-garden of their castle in the glen just at this time. It was warm, and the sun played on them as they sat there with a chess board between them. All around them the peaceful activities of the castle were in progress, and they could see and hear their people contentedly at work in the township that had grown about the castle.

But Naisi was oppressed and frowning, for he was suffering from a severe bout of homesickness for Ulster. His thoughts were not on the game and Deirdre was winning, even though she did not want to and ached within to comfort him.

She smiled at him encouragingly, but the look he returned was bitter; not with the reproach she read in it, but bitter for all that. And as she was about to ask him what ailed him, they heard the shout from far down the loch.

Naisi looked up, like a stag suddenly alert.

'That's the cry of an Ulsterman,' he said, his head cocked and his ears straining.

Deirdre too had heard the cry and moreover had recognised the voice which brought fear to her heart.

Quickly she replied: 'Don't be thinking wishfully, my love. It is only some poor Scotch hunter coming home late. Your move...'

And Naisi sank back in his seat and tried to play; but twice more Fergus hallooed, and each time nearer until at last Naisi sprang up and cried:

'It is an Ulsterman, and Fergus at that; Deirdre...'

But she stood up too and came beside him and laid her hand on his arm.

'I know,' she said, 'I knew it all the time, but Naisi...'

'But why didn't you say so?' he asked.

'Because,' she replied, 'last night I dreamt that three birds flew here to us from Emhain carrying a drop of honey each in their beaks which they left here with us; but when they flew away they took with them three drops of our blood.'

'And what do you think that means, my princess?' asked Naisi indulgently.

'That Fergus comes here with false message's of peace, sweet as honey; but he will take away with him three drops of blood,

114

you and Ainle and Ardan to your deaths.'

'Oh, nonsense,' cried Naisi, his heart bursting to see Fergus and hear from Ireland, 'above all others, we can trust Fergus... run down Ardan and show him the way here.'

And Ardan ran to the shore and the sight of Fergus and his two sons was to him like rain on the parched grass. He welcomed Fergus, and threw his arms around his neck and those of his sons and gave them three kisses and brought them to the castle.

There Naisi and Deirdre greeted them warmly and asked for news from home.

'The greatest news I have,' said Fergus, 'is that Conor has sent me to bring you back to Emhain and your place in the Red Branch and will restore your lands and property; I am myself a pledge for your safety.'

'There is no need for them to go,' said Deirdre, 'here they are as powerful as Conor is in Ulster.'

'To be in one's native land,' said Fergus, 'is better than power and prosperity elsewhere.'

'That is true,' said Naisi, 'for I would far rather be in Ireland, though I have more land and power here.'

But Deirdre was not so easily satisfied; the memory of her dream and her fear of the consequences, made her argue against return to Ireland from Alba where they were peaceful and happy.

'You need not worry,' said Fergus, 'I myself am the pledge and guardian of your safety.'

But still Deirdre tried to stop them. 'Do not go Naisi, do not go,' she cried, 'it is a trick. I know it, in my heart I know it.' And she began to lament and cry in great anguish so that it was hard for the four men to see it or to comfort her. Then Naisi said:

'Deirdre, my love, your fears are understandable, but... that is all. You know as well as I do that we can accept Fergus's word, and that is good enough for me. We'll go to-morrow.'

CHAPTER THREE

That night they spent in reminiscing and learning all the news from home from Fergus, who was amazed and impressed in his turn with what they had accomplished in this wild and uncultivated land. Only Deirdre remained quiet and while the night was still young she crept away to bed on the plea of a headache; but it was heartache that sickened her as she lay alone staring through the window of her room at the moon-drenched glen.

Next day they made their preparation's early and before the sun was high were sailing down the still loch towards the ocean and Ulster. The men stood gaily about the deck, craning forward to see ahead, but Deirdre alone sat in the stern and looked back towards Scotland; at the round, blue hills and wooded slopes, and in her heart she made this song:

> Dear land of Alba, I would not go
> From your green slopes beside the sea;
> My heavy heart is dull and slow
> To be abandoning your peace with Naisi.

> Dear glens I know and love so well
> Where he and I made love together;
> Hearing the cuckoo's summer spell
> And the hush of the snow clad winter heather.

> Dear to me your crystal water;
> Dear to me your sunlit sea;
> I'd never leave your welcome laughter
> Only to be with my love, Naisi.

Next day they sailed into the harbour beneath the fort of Borrach who was at the quayside to greet them. He welcomed them all with warm kisses and then, turning to Fergus, said:

'And for you, comrade, I have prepared a banquet which will last three days, so stay with me. But Conor wishes the sons of Usna to speed to Emhain Macha that he may welcome them with a banquet of his own.'

When Fergus heard this he became crimson with anger, and

116

said:

'You have done wrong, Borrach to invite me to a banquet knowing I cannot refuse; and knowing too that I am under obligation to bring the sons of Usna to Emhain under my protection without delay.'

But Borrach, who was in the king's confidence, insisted: 'It is the king's command,' he said, 'that you represent him here.'

Then Fergus asked Naisi what he should do, but it was Deirdre who answered for her husband.

'The choice is yours, Fergus, between a feast and the lives of the sons of Usna. They seem a high price to pay for a dinner.'

'I will not forsake them,' said Fergus, 'nor will I break my vow. I will stay here and my two sons, Illan the Fair and Buinne the Red will protect them and my honour.'

Then Naisi said, and he could not hide the contempt from his voice: 'We don't need your son's protection, Fergus; our own arms have always been enough protection for us.'

And so saying he walked away from Fergus in terrible anger, followed by Ainle and Ardan and Deirdre and Fergus's two sons. But Deirdre called Naisi and tried to persuade him not to go to Emhain Macha that night.

'Let's go to Cuchullain at Dun Dealgan,' she said, 'we can stay with him until it is time for Fergus to come with us to Emhain Macha.'

But the others would not agree, saying that it would look like cowardice on their part if they did so. And the sons of Fergus said that they would protect them as if they had been Fergus himself.

They reached Slieve Fuad and rested there for awhile, and as they were about to go on Naisi noticed that Deirdre was asleep. Gently he woke her, but when she saw him a look of terror crossed her face and she threw her arms around him and clung to him.

'What is it, my love,' he asked her, 'what is the matter?'

In grief and in fear she told him. 'I had a dream,' she said, 'I'm afraid.'

'Another one,' Naisi chided her gently, 'you are too apt to dream, love.'

But she clung to him while he tried to comfort her and said:

'I dreamt that I saw you and Ardan and Anile and Illan the Fair headless and bloody, but there was Buinne the Red without a mark on his body.'

'Hush,' said Naisi, 'hush. It was only a dream.'

'Oh Naisi,' she cried, 'I'm frightened. Let's not go to Emhain.

But Naisi thought, so terribly upset was Deirdre, that weariness and terror had made her distraught and only pressed on all the harder so that she might get rest, in spite of all her protests.

'Look,' she cried as they approached, 'even over the city there hangs a bloody cloud. Isn't that omen enough for you.'

But Naisi was too worried about her to listen to what she said, for he loved her greatly.

Then she said in a quieter voice.

'Naisi, there is one test by which you will know if Conor is planning harm to us or not. If he welcomes us into his palace, then everything is all right, for no king will harm a guest in his own house; but if he sends you elsewhere, then he means treachery.'

Well then, when they reached the city they were met at the gates by a messenger from Conor to light them through the streets, and who said to them:

'Conor bids you welcome, and for this night would ask you to share the hospitality of the House of the Red Branch where a banquet awaits you.'

And he began to lead them towards the House of the Red Branch. Deirdre said to Naisi:

'It is as I said, he is planning some treachery, let us go somewhere else.'

But Naisi said no, that there was nowhere more fitting for the champions of the Red Branch to spend the night than in the House of the Red Branch, and he said this to comfort her, for he was annoyed that the king did not take them to the palace. And Illan the Fair said: 'The sons of Fergus have never showed cowardliness or unmanliness, and we will not show it now.'

So they were taken to the House of the Red Branch where a banquet was spread for them. But neither Deirde nor Naisi were interested in food; he because he was worried about her, and she because she feared Conor. So Naisi called for a chessboard, and said:

'You remember the last game we played in Scotland and you beat me. Well, now that we are home again, I'll beat you.'

118

And he smiled lovingly at her.

But Deirdre did not smile back, for a great heaviness and terror for what might happen soon was weighing on her heart, and in her mind she felt that there was not long more for them to enjoy.

Meantime Conor sat in his palace brooding with impatience at the thought that Deirdre was so near and yet unattainable. So he called Leabharcam, who was still alive, and said to her:

'Go and see if Deirdre is still as lovely as when you reared her, for if so there is not on the ridge of the world a woman more beautiful.'

But Leabharcam still retained her great love for Deirdre and when she reached the House of the Red Branch they fell into each others arms. She greeted Deirdre and Naisi with kisses and tears mixed; with laughter and with lamentation, and among her warm greetings she warned them of what Conor planned.

'Childeen,' she said to Deirdre, 'be careful; and you Naisi, and your brothers and the sons of Fergus too, be careful. For this night there is evil planned in Emhain, and I know that the Three Torches of Valour of the Gael are to be assailed and attacked and killed. So guard well and fight well and defend well that ye may last until Fergus comes.'

Then she went back to the king, and Conor asked her for her news.

'I have good news,' she said, 'and bad news. And the good news is that the three sons of Usna, the three valiant cham-

So Trendorn went down to the House of the Red Branch, but when he found the great doors and windows barred and bolted, he became afraid that the sons of Usna were waiting for him or one like him, so he climbed to a small window high in the wall and looked through.

Naisi and Deirdre were still playing chess, but as Trendorn looked in Deirdre happened to glance up and seeing the face at the window let out a gasp. Naisi following her eyes, flung the chessman he had in his hand at the window with all his force and struck Trendorn in the eye with it, so hard, that it blew the eyeball from its socket and Trendorn fell back to the ground.

Then Trendorn returned to Conor and told him what had happened. This suited Conor admirably for, in the appearance of great anger, he rushed into the palace hall where some of his nobles were and cried: 'The man who has maimed my servant would himself be king.'

He had already learned from Trendorn that Deirdre was as beautiful as ever and he let his jealousy work on his wrath until he roused his troops crying that the sons of Usna had tried to kill Trendorn.

He rushed out of his palace and ordered a battalion of mercenary troops that were standing by in the yard to attack the Red Branch House at once, capture the sons of Usna and bring them to him for punishment.

And the troops attacked the House and tried to set it on fire. But the great oaken doors withstood their siege. Then Buinne _ _ _ _ _ _ _ _ _ _ _ _ said: 'It is my place to go out and fight.

stopped the fighting. The terrible noise that is like no other noise died away the way thunder dies away across a hill, and the men stood back from each other warily and breathless. Conor looked closely at Buinne; the heavy face, the determined clenched hand on his sword, and called him over. Buinne came stalking over, his heavy sword still dripping blood held out before him as he came up to the king.

Without preliminary Conor said: 'Buinne, you do not know what you are about, fighting me. I have given your father a thousand acres of land and ten cattle for each acre; you'll get the same if you'll fight with me against these traitors.'

Buinne merely shook his head and turned to go. But when he turned his back upon the king and faced again the black and armed hosts he fought, and every face a warriors face, and every spear full ten feet long and every arm a strong arm and every sword gleam dull and bright along its centre where no blood as yet had run along the ridged blade, he knew that he must die. He knew that the sons of Usna, too, must die, and that they'd die in any case if he should die or not. So he spoke to the king and said:

'I will do that.'

And when Deirdre saw him join the throng she cried: 'Buinne has deserted you, Naisi; like father like son.'

'But he did good work before he left,' said Naisi. By now the king's mercenaries were thundering at the door again, and Illan the Fair said:

'If Fergus was a traitor, and Buinne was a traitor, then I will not be one as long as this straight sword is in my hand; I will not forsake the sons of Usna.'

Then the doors were thrown open and Illan the Fair and his men rushed out and made three swift onslaughts on the hosts of Conor round the House of the Red Branch, and slew and killed three hundred of his men and then rushed in again between the mighty doors held open for the purpose.

Inside were Deirdre and her husband still intent upon their game, for the champions and their wives would never show a sign of fear or of alarm; and calmed their hearts as if it was nothing but a wind that raged outside. Again the troops of Conor thronged about and tried to fire the ancient House and out upon them like a lion rushed Illan, destroying their work and them in one red rout. Then Conor, who had seen it all, enquired who this young hero was and when he heard, said: 'Fiachra, my son, both you and Illan were born on the same night. Take my shield, Ocean, Flight, my spear and Victory, my sword, and vanquish him before he does more harm.'

And Fiachra went and so they fought a fair and warlike, red and bloody, manly, bitter, savage, hot and vehement, terrible battle with each other between the silent hosts of men who, in the flickering torchlight and from the fires that glowed where battle had incendiarised the city streets, looked on. Till Illan in a sudden twist hurled Fiachra to the ground so that the royal king's son was forced to crouch beneath the shield, the Ocean. And it was also called the Moaner because in battle it was known that the king's shield moaned when he who wore it was in danger, no matter if it were the king himself or one of his own blood; and if he were in fear of death the moan was heard across the face of Ireland and was answered by the Three Great Moaning Waves of Erin; the Wave of Tuatha at the Bann, the Wave of Rory in the Bay of Dundrum and the Wave of Cliona in Glandore.

And so it moaned. And when from some far distance Conall Cearnach heard the moan, he thought it was the king himself who lay in danger and rushed fiercely to the spot and, without pausing to see who it was attacked the man beneath the shelter of the Moaner, struck him from behind.

'Ah,' cried Illan the Fair, 'who struck me from behind when he might have had fair battle had he sought it?'

'And who are you,' cried Conall, for he still didn't recognise him, 'to attack the king.'

'Illan the son of Fergus – and you are Conall Cearnach – and you have done wrong to kill me while I am defending the sons of Usna who are in the Red Branch House under my father's protection.'

'By God,' cried Conall, 'you will not go unavenged.' And lifting his sword he struck the head from Fiachra below his beard. Then he turned in grief and rage and stalked fierce and silent from the battlefield.

Illan, dying within the circle of his enemies, called to Naisi to defend himself bravely; and then, with his remaining strength, he flung his arms into the House of the Red Branch so that the victors would not have them, and the shadow of death fell on him and he died.

Now another great battalion of mercenaries attacked the House of the Red Branch and tried to fire it with burning faggots. And Ainle sallied forth and held them back a while, and then came Ardan to relieve him, and finally Naisi came himself and fought with them until the morning's dawn and so terrible was the slaughter that they made, the sons of Usna, on the hired hosts of Conor that he feared his army would be spoiled; for until the seashore sands and all the forest leaves; the gleaming dew-drops on the morning grass or the firey stars of night are calculated, then it would not be possible to tabulate the heads and hands, the severed legs and sundered limbs that there lay red and bloody at the hands of Naisi and his brothers.

Finally the three heroes and their few followers made a phalanx with Deirdre in its centre and swept down upon the ranks of Conor. When the king saw what was happening he called Catha, the druid, and said:

'It would be better for us if these three heroes fought for us rather than against us. With their few followers they have near decimated my army, and I would willingly receive them back into my service. Go to them and bring them to me under my pledge that no harm will befall them.'

And Catha, by no means distrusting the king, for his face was earnest and in his deep brown eyes the sombreness of truth looked out at him intensely, went and raised a mighty wood before them, through which they thought no man could pass, so black and tangled were its limbs. But without paus-

the sons of Usna.

He conjured up a great morass, a bog of green and brown that clung about their feet and dragged them down and clogged their limbs so that they could not move. Then to where they stood, held fast in the bog, the men of Ulster ran, for they were not affected by the spell, and bound them with chains. Then Catha raised the spell, and reminded the king of his promised word. But Conor laughed at him and told him he was an old man who didn't understand the art of diplomacy.

Then the king called loudly, a smile of triumph on his face, for one of his men to kill the sons of Usna. But no man came. He called again and still no one came to do it. And a third time he called and as he called his anger grew in him, because he knew why they would not come. Turning to where they stood, Deirdre standing beside Naisi, holding his hand bound as it was with iron, the king cursed and swore at them, but got no answer other than a steady look from each, more kingly than he ever owned himself.

But in the household of the king a son of Lochlann's king called Mainni Rough Hand lived, half savage and half wild and willing to do anything he was bidden. The king sent for him whose brothers Naisi had some years before killed in battle, and this man undertook to kill the sons of Usna.

Then, with a grin of pleasure on his face, this Mainni stooped to where the sword of Naisi – a heritage from Mananaan – lay fallen on the grass. He swung it so it sang above his head, then quicker than the eye might follow him he turned com-

Without my love I can't abide,
So dig the grave both deep and wide.

The hawks of the mountain are flown
And I am left to weep alone.
My grief the turning world would cover
Until I lie with my true lover.

I am Deirdre the joyless
For a short time alive
Though to end life be evil
It is worse to survive.'

Then Conor had her brought to Emhain Macha by force, and for a year she lived there, but no smile or laugh or any sign of living stirred in her for all that time. And finally, when he grew tired of her disdain and found that he did not, in truth, love her at all, Conor decided to taunt her and try to get some satisfaction that way, and provoke her anger by his cruelty.

So he said to her: 'What is it Deirdre, that you hate above all things on this earth?'

And she replied: 'You yourself, and Eoghan of Durracht' – which was the name and title Conor had bestowed on Mainni for his job as executioner.

And Conor smiled and said, 'Well, in that case, since you have spent a year with me in Emhain, it is only right that you should spend another year with him in Durracht.'

Then, wasting no time, he ordered that his chariot should be harnessed to the swiftest horses in the yard. Now this cruelty of his was no accident, for Mainni, or Eoghan as he now preferred to be called, was standing near them all this time; and it was perhaps the remembrance of what had passed between the three of them a year before that moved Conor to this final act of perverted passion.

All this time while waiting for the horses Conor smiled, and Eoghan smiled; but Deirdre never smiled. And when it was ready the three of them with the driver mounted the great chariot and drove to Durracht, Deirdre sitting between Conor and the lasciviously smiling Eoghan. Across the hills of Emhain they charged at a gallop, the black clods of the earth flying like birds flocking behind them, thrown up by the stampeding feet of the horses.

Then Conor turned to Deirdre and she looked back at him, so that his eye dropped; but it passed on to Eoghan, and she followed his look. And from some great malice in him Conor spoke, just as they were passing the grave of the sons of Usna;

'Deirdre,' he said, 'the look you pass between Eoghan and myself is like the hot look of a ewe between two rams.'

Then, with a cry, Deirdre sprang up and leaped out of the chariot, smashing her head against the stone that rose above the grave of the Three Lights of Valour of the Gael, Naisi, Ainle and Ardan. And when they buried her, in the same grave which she had asked be dug for four and not for three, her arm fell round the neck of Naisi where he lay as fresh as on the day he died, and on his mouth her mouth rested, and so they were buried in the one tomb. And all the men of Ulster. who stood by wept aloud.

And from their grave there grew two straight and slender trees of yew, the branches and the leaves of which entwined and made an arch above.

This, then, is the story of Deirdre and the Sons of Usna. And when Fergus had freed himself from Borracht's banquet and found that the sons of Usna had been slain and himself dishonoured, he left the court of Conor in a mighty rage and, with all his people returned again to Connacht.

There, mindful of his word at last, in a fire of immense rage, he gathered all the warlike hosts of Maeve and made war on Ulster. And Catha, who indeed was the grandfather of the sons of Usna, for they were his daughter's children, cursed king Conor that none of his breed might ever rule in Emhain Macha again. And so it was, for when the mightiest of the heros died, Cuchullain strapped against a pillared rock and stood alone to face the warring hordes of Maeve, then Emhain fell, and overgrew with great and waving tufts of grass.

126

THE SECOND BOOK OF IRISH MYTHS AND LEGENDS

by Eoin Neeson

Again more fascinating tales are contained in this follow up to *The First Book of Irish Myths and Legends.*

Included in this most readable and interesting work is *The Children of Lir,* a fanciful, half other world tale that has a good deal of poignancy and considerable literary merit. There is also the great epic of the Fenian cycle, *Diarmuid and Graine* which is to its time and place what *Helen and Paris* is to the *Iliad.* The third story is about the hero Cuchulain, probably the greatest symbol of heroism associated with Ireland. However in this tale his honour emerges in a doubtful light because of the manner in which he treats the women who love him.

The exaggeratedly recognisable human traits and the sophisticated concepts of human behaviour painted with such skill and acute observation are far ahead of their time in Western Europe.

THE BEDSIDE BOOK OF IRISH FABLES AND LEGENDS

by Maureen Donegan

In this fascinating book of Irish legends the reader will meet many old friends from Ireland's distant past. Head and shoulders above them all is Cuchulainn, whose birth was surrounded with mystery and whose life was full of battles and love, enchantment and treachery. Maureen Donegan traces his career from the precocious child through his lusty youth to the proud middle-aged, battled-scarred hero.

We also meet the Lupracans, the miniature water sprites who live under the sea, Fergus and the Monster, Fionn and the Gilla Dacker and discover how Diarmuid got his Love-Spot. We see them struggling with life, sometimes helped by a bit of magic but as often hindered by it. They may be larger than life but they are overwhelmingly and endearingly human.

IN IRELAND LONG AGO

Kevin Danaher

Those who have only the most hazy ideas about how our ancestors lived in Ireland will find enlightnment in these essays which range widely over the field of Irish Folklife. Kevin Danaher describes life in Ireland before the 'brave new world' crept into the quiet countryside. Or perhaps 'describe' is not the right word. He rather invites the reader to call on the elderly people at their homes, to listen to their tales and gossip and taste their food and drink; to step outside and marvel at their pots and pans, plough and flails; to meet a water diviner; to join a faction fight; hurry to a wedding and bow down in remembrance of the dead.

Not only does the author write about people with reverence but those people are reverently introduced to the reader by their own words, as when the Kerryman replied to the Dublin man who asked him if he could take a photograph of his donkey with the baskets. 'You never saw one before?' Oh man, you must be from a very backward part of the country!'

In this book Kevin Danaher has not only given us a well balanced picture of life in Ireland, but has also gone far to capture the magic of the written word.

FOLKTALES OF THE IRISH COUNTRYSIDE

Kevin Danaher

Nowdays there is a whole generation grownig up who cannot remember a time when there was no television; and whose parents cannot remember a time when there was no radio and cinema. It is not, therefore, surprising that many of them wonder what people in country places found to do with their time in the winters of long ago.

People may blink in astonishment when reminded of the fact that the night was too often too short for those past generations of country people, whose own entertainment with singing, music, dancing, cards, indoor games, and storytelling spanned the evenings and into morning light.

Kevin Danaher, a member of the Irish Folklore Commission staff, remembers forty of the stories that enlivened those past days. Some are stories told by members of his own family; others he took down in his own countryside from the last of the traditional storytellers. Included are stories of giants, of ghosts, of wondrous deeds, queer happenings, of the fairies and the great kings of Ireland who had beautiful daughters and many problems.

A homely, heartwarming collection of tales that spring naturally from the heart of the Irish Countryside.